D0622590

LIVING

THE INFINITE

WAY

WRITINGS OF JOEL S. GOLDSMITH

The Thunder of Silence
The Art of Spiritual Healing
The Art of Meditation
Practicing the Presence
The Infinite Way
Living The Infinite Way
Spiritual Interpretation of Scripture
The Letters
The Master Speaks
Conscious Union with God
Consciousness Unfolding
God the Substance of All Form
Infinite Way Letters 1954
Infinite Way Letters 1955
Infinite Way Letters 1956
Infinite Way Letters 1957
Infinite Way Letters 1958
Infinite Way Letters 1959

LIVING

THE INFINITE

WAY

Revised Edition

BY JOEL S. GOLDSMITH

HARPER & ROW, PUBLISHERS
New York, Evanston, and London

Library of Congress catalog card number: 61–9646

Except the Lord build the house, they
labour in vain that build it.
—Psalm 127

Illumination dissolves all material ties and binds men
together with the golden chains of spiritual understanding; it acknowledges only the leadership of the Christ;
it has no ritual or rule but the divine, impersonal universal Love, no other worship than the inner Flame
that is ever lit at the shrine of Spirit. This union is the
free state of spiritual brotherhood. The only restraint
is the discipline of Soul; therefore, we know liberty
without license; we are a united universe without physical limits, a divine service to God without ceremony
or creed. The illumined walk without fear—by Grace.

—THE INFINITE WAY

CONTENTS

INTRODUCTION

One of the greatest spiritual teachers who ever walked this earth has told us that man does not live by bread alone, but by every word that proceedeth out of the mouth of God. Throughout every age there have been men and women of discernment who have discovered that this is true. Some have left a testament of their discovery in the scriptures of the world—a record of courage, strength, and inspiration, a revelation of unfolding consciousness. The experience of these illumined men and women is a constant reminder that we do not live merely by work, food, and rest, but that there is another factor that enters life which is far more important than any of these human activities. This factor is the "word that proceedeth out of the mouth of God."

The Word becomes the living waters. It is our protection, our safety, our security. As we go about our tasks and duties, even though we may go through deep waters and be tried in the fire of experience, the waters will not overflow us and the flames will not kindle upon us, if the word of God is in us and with us. It is our meat, our water, and our bread of life, our staff on which to lean. But the Word must be more than a quotation from a book. It must come alive within us; it must be a vital, living force. Its essence or substance must become part of our own consciousness, no longer words, but the Word. Then it lives and functions for us eternally.

What is there about a Bible that is holy? Is it the binding, the paper, the print, or the words? Not one of these is sacred. The only thing in the entire Bible that is power is the word of God. And where do we find that? In a book? No, for then it would be necessary merely to buy the book to have the word of God. Millions of people buy the Bible every year, but how many of these people have the word of God? Most of them have some words printed in a book. The world has missed the mark by reading the Bible as a historical or literary work. As long as it remains print in a book, it does not become flesh. The Word is within our mouth, within our consciousness, within our Soul, and it is there that it becomes flesh and dwells among us.

The Bible is the Book of Life. When its teachings are spiritually discerned, it is filled with the very bread of life, the very water, and the very wine. As a book it is not our protection nor our security. Be assured of this: If we memorized the entire Bible from Genesis to Revelation, we might still find ourselves "an hungered," sick, and lonely. Only as the Word takes root in consciousness can it come forth as flesh, as demonstration.

It is of little value, for example, to repeat the Ninety-first Psalm, and to think that because of continued repetition we shall be protected by its teachings. It is when we have fulfilled the requirement of the Ninety-first Psalm, by dwelling in the "secret place of the most High," by abiding in spiritual truth, by living in the continuous recognition of God as the only Cause and creative Principle, that it becomes operative in our experience. When we dwell in this truth so that it becomes the very embodiment of our being, we no longer have any fear. The truth in which we are abiding, and which we are permitting to abide in us, becomes our fortress; it becomes our rock; and we come to a place in consciousness where we realize that this truth is our shield and buckler, our fortress, our very good itself.

Scripture plays a greater and greater part in our lives as its inner meaning unfolds and reveals itself. All Scripture must be interpreted spiritually in order to penetrate the depth of its message. Pondering and meditating on the Word will reveal its real meaning or essence, and then it "is quick, and powerful, and sharper than any two-edged sword." The mind yields from its intellectual base to its spiritual base, and God is revealed as a present possibility.

The written or spoken word is the least important part of our work. That which is not written or spoken is the real teaching. In the Bible this teaching is called "the pearl of great price." When we find this pearl, the particular teaching that says to us, "This is for me; this is the way," then let us follow it. When the unfoldment or revelation of God has come to our consciousness, and we have touched even the hem of the Robe, we shall no longer need books or teachers.

Inner unfoldment is the mission of The Infinite Way. Its purpose is the revelation of truth from within our own being and the attainment of a conscious awareness of the presence of God. It is not so much a teaching as an experience, an experience of the Christ, a God-experience.

The Master gave us the illustration of planting the seed in fertile soil, in stony soil, and in barren soil. It is the seed planted in fertile soil that springs up into fruitage. How can we recognize fertile soil? How can we know when our consciousness is fertile for the planting of the word of Truth? We may be sure that it is stony and barren so long as it is concerned with outer results. The only time our consciousness is fertile for planting the spiritual seed is when we can say, "I am seeking only spiritual fruitage, spiritual harmony, spiritual health, spiritual wealth, spiritual companionship." When we can be satisfied to let the kingdom of God interpret itself to us in its own language and not in accordance with what we think our needs or requirements are, then, and then only, is consciousness seeking spiritual fruitage.

After the seed is planted in our consciousness, there comes the same period of gestation as comes with the development of the child, and there is the period of growth and unfoldment. In the spiritual kingdom, there is no such process, but because we are not at the standpoint of absolute readiness for instantaneous ascension, we must pass through the same period of preliminary unfoldment as did the Master. To him came the awakening, the three-year ministry, the three temptations in the wilderness, the Garden of Gethsemane, the Crucifixion, the Resurrection, and then the final and complete revelation of God as his very own being, in which he ascended above all material sense of body. Up to that point his experience was one of unfoldment.

In the same way with each one of us, there must be a preparation for the planting of the seed. The first preparation is the renunciation of material achievement, the decision as to whom we shall serve—God or mammon, God or results. When we come to the point of renunciation, where we are willing to give up all and "follow Me," we find the mystery and the miracle. Nothing real has been sacrificed, and all has been gained.

We must become "the new man," and this is achieved as an activity of consciousness. If there is no change in our consciousness, there will be no change in our outer experience, because that which is in consciousness comes forth as manifestation. There is not Truth and manifestation: Truth appears as manifestation. Spirit is not something separate and apart from the forms it assumes: Spirit is the substance and the form of Its manifestation. The Truth revealed in secret appears as manifested form.

Our purpose, therefore, in being on this Path is the expansion of consciousness, the revelation of the new man—the Son of God. Our unfoldment depends upon what we are seeking. Are we seeking only the demonstration of God? Are we ready at this moment to stop taking thought for the things of this world, which are no part of the spiritual kingdom, and realize: "All I want is the kingdom of God on earth. I desire only the kingdom of God, the reign of God in my individual experience, the government of God in my individual affairs."

When we are ready to do this, to die daily to a limited human life and to be reborn of the Spirit, we are no longer limited to a human mind or to a human experience. Spirit knows no limitation. Spirit just pours Itself through. It comes flowing through in such a glorious, rushing manner that we can scarcely believe it. It may flow through as an entirely new life, as new work, as new activity, or it may increase and prosper that in which we are already engaged. We become beholders of the activity of God and marvel at its munificence, its beauty, and its bounty. In that moment of heightened awareness, we know there is a high purpose for each one of us, a divine destiny.

Spiritual living is a life lived by Grace, not by might nor by power, a life in which we find all things appearing to us in the order in which we need them, sometimes before we ourselves are aware of that need. This is living by Grace and it is attained only when things, thoughts, and desires have been overcome. We have not overcome the world while we are trying to improve or increase our material sense of the world. Spiritual life is that state of being in which we live by Grace, in which we know that, whatever the need is, the answer will appear. Everything that comes, comes as the gift of God. As a matter of fact, it comes just a little bit before we need it, even before we know we are going to need it. A path opens before us of indescribable beauty, joy, and peace.

Remember that from now on we do not live by bread alone; we do not live by money; we do not live by human rest: We live by the Word brought into our thought and into our remembrance. Here is the great secret. From the moment we begin to take the word of God into our thought secretly and silently, telling no one, a change begins to take place in us. From that moment, the great secret of life is ours, the secret found in all scripture spiritually discerned, the secret which the Master tried to impart to us two thousand years ago: "The kingdom of God is within you." When we realize the kingdom of God as revealed through the word of God, it becomes evident and vital in our experience as our body, as our being, as our mind, and as our Soul.

The word of God is the great truth that becomes flesh, that becomes tangible in our lives. This Word held close within us, thought upon, dwelt upon, remembered, becomes the spiritual activity of life and brings spiritual qualities into expression. There is no way to bring a spiritual good, a spiritual power, into our experience from outside our own being. Spirituality is not something that comes to us, but rather something that flows out from us, when we entertain the Word within. "If ye abide in me, and my words abide in you," then the great peace, the great delights of this world, will be yours. No evil will come to you, and there will be nothing for you to fear.

Every day take the Word into your consciousness, and as often as possible throughout the day remind yourself of it. If you do that, you will never again be quite the same because from that moment on, it is as if you had touched an infinite Center of wisdom or knowledge, an infinite Presence that directs, protects, maintains, and sustains. Those of you who are on this Path and who have not yet had this experience, will achieve it, because it is written: "Ye have not chosen me, but I have chosen you." God has brought you to this place of unfoldment and will not suffer you to stray from the path until you have received your illumination. The Way lies open before you.

JOEL S. GOLDSMITH
Box 5308 Pawaa Station
Honolulu, Hawaii

LIVING

THE INFINITE

WAY

CHAPTER I

THE MYSTERY OF THE INVISIBLE

All through the ages men have sought to understand the mystery of life. They have searched for that something called the secret of life, particularly the secret of success and happiness; and like those who sought for the Holy Grail, they have looked for it every place in the world except where it is to be found.

The truly successful people of life are not readily identified because, while it is easy to find the person who has acquired the most millions or the one who has gained the greatest fame in some area, it is not always easy to find those who have attained real success. Success should bring happiness, and especially inner peace and security, and so true success means something far different from the mere acquisition of things or the attainment of personal power or glory.

Spiritual living may carry with it just as much of fame

and fortune as material living, but these are acquired, first of all, not as the goal, but as the added things, and secondly, not from without, but from within through an understanding of their Source. In material living, whatever can be gained from without is of necessity limited, but there is absolutely no limit to the attainment of a person who has discovered the secret of the inner life. Therein lies the difference between material and spiritual living.

The secret of the inner life is revealed through meditation which, in its earliest stages, is an act of conscious awareness whereby we make contact with an area of consciousness within ourselves which is actually the storehouse of our lives.

There was a time when man was pure, spiritual being, when he lived entirely from within himself, when his thoughts always remained at the center of his being, and life flowed out from within—ideas came from within, means of action came from within, and whenever there was an apparent need, all that he had to do was to close his eyes, go within, and let it come forth into expression.

We have no actual knowledge of this period or of its ending, but we do know that the Bible symbolically relates the story of Adam and Eve who lived a divinely spiritual life without a problem, but who were compelled to leave the Garden of Eden and thereafter experienced all the troubles of human living—materialistic living. We are told that the reason for this fall from Grace was the acceptance of the belief in two powers—good and evil.[1]

[1] For a detailed exposition of this subject, see the author's *The Thunder of Silence* (New York: Harper & Brothers, 1961).

It was an act of consciousness and, despite the commonly accepted theological interpretation, was not in any way related to sex.

The Garden of Eden episode contains a lesson in living for all of us. How often we feel that our lives are made or marred by some external act, but this is never true because it is always something that takes place within our consciousness that brings about the change for good or evil, and in the allegory of Adam and Eve, the downfall of man is explained as the acceptance of the belief in good and evil.

Another symbolic story in Scripture is that of the prodigal son. Here, the son of the king, who in and of himself was nothing, but who as the heir of the king was not only regal but wealthy, decided to cut himself off from the source of his good, that is, from his Father's house, his Father-consciousness. Taking the substance which he felt was his due, he began to live on that finite and limited amount that he had received. Living thus finitely, he cut himself off from his Source. Whatever money he spent left him with that much less; every day of life he lived found him with a day less to live; every bit of strength or substance that he used found him with that much less, because he was using the substance that he had without being able to replenish it from the Source from which he had cut himself off by his own act.

That same principle is brought out in the lesson of the vine and the branches which the Master gave to his disciples in the fifteenth chapter of John:

I am the vine, ye are the branches: He that abideth in me,

and I in him, the same bringeth forth much fruit: for without me ye can do nothing.

If a man abide not in me, he is cast forth as a branch, and is withered; and men gather them, and cast them into the fire, and they are burned.

Herein lies the essence of biblical wisdom: Cut off from the vine, the branch withers, no longer having access to the Source; cut off from the Father's house, or consciousness, the prodigal consorts with the swine; cut off from their Source and expelled from the Garden of Eden, Adam and Eve are compelled to live on their own substance.

In all three illustrations, there is the one spiritual lesson: When we are cut off from the Source of our being, we are using up our own life—our own mind, strength, health, wisdom, guidance, and direction—and eventually we come to that period when we are withered. On the other hand, by maintaining our contact with the vine, by maintaining our relationship with the Father as the son or heir, or by remaining in Eden, in the kingdom of God, we draw on the infinite Storehouse. This way leads to eternality, immortality, infinity, harmony, completeness, and perfection.

As human beings living a materialistic life in the world, we are the branch that is cut off from the tree; we are the prodigal without a Father; we are that Adam expelled from the Garden. Living such a life, there is no God-government, God-protection, or God-sustenance. Infants, children, young men, and young women suffer and die; the aged are infirm, decrepit, and worn out be-

cause from the cradle to the grave there is a sense of separation from their Source.

The truth is that it is not possible to pray to God and
thus receive the benefits of God; it is not possible to be
just a good man or woman—even a churchgoing man or
woman—and thereby have contact with God, because the
contact with God is not made in any external way. The
whole world has been, and is, riding to hell all the while
it is praying to God to save it, but never getting any
answer!

That is why, in this age, the entire world is seeking an
answer to this riddle, and many are seeking it through
prayer and meditation. There can be no peace within or
without until there is an abiding in the Word and letting
the Word abide in us, a returning to the Father's house
through this inner contact and drawing our substance,
not from one another, not by preying upon one another,
nor by falsely advertising our wares to deceive one another, but by drawing upon the substance which is of the
Father.

Is not the whole secret of life contained and summed
up in that brief conversation which took place between
the Master and his disciples just after Jesus had missed
his midday meal? He had been giving a lesson to the
woman at the well of Samaria, and the disciples "prayed
him, saying, Master, eat."

And do you remember his answer? "I have meat to eat
that ye know not of."

This was much the same answer that he gave to the
woman at the well when she asked, "Sir, thou hast nothing to draw with, and the well is deep: from whence then

hast thou that living water?" How indeed could he do this?

But he explained that he had water, wellsprings of it, and "whosoever drinketh of the water that I shall give him shall never thirst; but the water that I shall give him shall be in him a well of water springing up into everlasting life." And later to the multitudes seeking food, the Master said, "I am the bread of life: he that cometh to me shall never hunger; and he that believeth on me shall never thirst." And to Thomas, "I am the way, the truth, and the life."

He was teaching that within us is embodied all that is necessary for our life and for our unfoldment—for our business, companionship, and supply. Within us, through the grace of God, the Father speaks, "Son, thou art ever with me, and all that I have is thine"—*all* that *I*[2] have! Where is this Father? Where is this "all that I have"? And the Master says, "Within you—the kingdom of God is within you." The kingdom of God, the allness of God, is within us!

And so we learn the mystery of life: We learn that if we are to tap the infinite Storehouse, if we are to draw to ourselves infinite good, infinite harmony, abundance, wholeness, perfection, completeness, joy, satisfaction, safety, and security, it is necessary to draw these out from within our own being.

To the human being, taught to look outside of himself, and even in his prayers to look up to heaven, or to look at a crucifix, a star, or some other symbol, it comes as a strange revelation that not only is there nothing out

---

[2] Wherever "I" is italicized, the reference is to God.

there, but there is no need of there being anything out there. Even if there were, we would have no need of it, because "I have meat to eat that ye know not of. [*I* can give you water, living water, even without a bucket, even without a well.] I am the way, the truth, and the life"— I am He, and all that is, is within me.

The only way that this meat, wine, and water can be drawn out into visible expression is by making contact with that inner Source. We are not accustomed to the idea that all that we are seeking is already embodied within us; we are not familiar enough with Jesus' promises; we have not lived with His words and teaching long enough: "Son, thou art ever with me, and all that I have is thine." Where? Within us! Within our own consciousness.

So it is that, as we learn to meditate and discover this kingdom within, a great mystery begins to reveal itself. When we stop to think about it, we cannot help but realize that everything in the world that we have ever feared is external to our own being, whether it is a person or an army, whether bullets or poison, climate, weather, or storms; whether it is a fear of being up in the air or down in the ocean—regardless of what it is that we have feared or are fearing, it is always something external to us. The first secret, therefore, that we learn in meditation, the very first revelation that comes to us, is that all power is within us and that there is no external power that can act upon us.

The Master said to Pilate, "Thou couldest have no power at all against me, except it were given thee from above"; and yet Pilate was the great temporal power of his day. The Master said to the storm, "Peace, be still," and it was still; to the palsied man, "Arise, take up thy bed, and go unto thine house," and he did; to the man with the withered hand, "Stretch forth thine hand," and it was restored.

The teaching of the Master is a whole new revelation that the kingdom of God, the kingdom of power, is within—that all power is within. This is an entirely new concept, and therefore, the very first step that we have to take in spiritual living is to realize that the kingdom of God is established within us, and secondly, to recognize that all that we have feared, even when it has come to us under the guise of law—material or mental law—is not power.

Now Scripture becomes understandable and meaningful. God gave dominion to us. He did not give it to the stars, the weather, or the climate. God did not give power or dominion to the poisons, the infections, and the contagions in the world; God did not give power to bullets and bombs: God gave us dominion over all that exists between heaven and hell—up or down, in or out.

Those who live the spiritual life do not become, or permit themselves to become, victims of circumstances, conditions, or people outside their own being, nor need they be beneficiaries of any activity, person, or thing external to themselves. If, and in proportion as, they live in the realization, "Son, thou art ever with me, and all that I have is thine," they develop their unique capacities, whether these be spiritual capacities, or capacities in architectural, musical, artistic, mechanical, or commercial fields.

So it is that gradually we learn that our own consciousness when it is imbued with Truth becomes the law of harmony unto our entire experience. "Whatsoever a man soweth, that shall he also reap. . . . and with what measure ye mete, it shall be measured to you again"—thus indicating that our experience unfolds from within our own being. It is an invisible law that that which the Father seeth in secret is shouted from the housetops.

If we have determined upon a life as a musician, artist, sculptor, or architect, we would discover, with this Truth, that we do not have to go outside and advertise to make ourselves known, but that automatically, invisibly, spiritually, we draw to ourselves those of our own state of consciousness, those whom we can bless and those who can bless us.

There is an invisible bond existing among all of us. There is an invisible bond between you and all those who represent the state of consciousness in which you find yourself. There is an invisible bond between me and all those who are attuned to the state of consciousness I represent, so that if I want to function as a spiritual teacher or practitioner, I need never announce it—I need only sit quietly in my own home and wait for the world to beat a pathway to my doorstep.

In living the life of the Spirit, there is no longer any blame for untoward events attached to persons or circumstances external to us, and those who become avenues or instruments for good to us are recognized as instruments of God. It is the divine principle using them to bring this good to us, and God, Itself,[3] is the Source.

[3] In the spiritual literature of the world, the varying concepts of God

Adam and Eve, the prodigal, the branch that is cut off from the vine—all of these became what they were because they had separated themselves from their Source. And remember that the discords and inharmonies, the sins, the diseases, and the poverties that we experience are due to our having been cut off from our Source, and the remedy lies in once more traveling back to the Father's house.

This we do through the recognition that that which I am seeking, I am and have, that all that the Father has is mine, and that "man shall not live by bread alone"— man shall not live by anything external—"but by every word that proceedeth out of the mouth of God." Again, it is something within our own being that is responsible for our destiny.

So it is that as we turn to the spiritual way of life we learn to depend less and less on persons, places, things, circumstances, and conditions; we learn to fear less every activity or form external to our being; we begin to abide in this Word and recognize that the kingdom of God is within us and that all that the Father has is ours. When this takes place, one day in our meditation we shall hear the words that will set us free, set us free from all outer discords and inharmonies, from all the trials and tribulations of this world. Then we, too, will be able to say with Jesus, "I have overcome the world," and we shall hear a word in our ears:

---

are indicated by the use of such words as "Father," "Mother," "Soul," "Spirit," "Principle," "Love," and "Life." Therefore, in this book, the author has used the pronouns "He" and "It," or "Himself" and "Itself," interchangeably in referring to God.

"*I will never leave thee, nor forsake thee. . . . lo, I am
with you alway, even unto the end of the world.*" *I am
thy bread, thy wine, thy water, and thy meat.*

*I am thy life eternal; I am thy immortal being; I am
even the resurrection, so that if thy body, thy home, and
thy supply were destroyed—if all these were destroyed—
I will raise them up. Just give Me a few days, and I in
the midst of thee will raise them up.*

*I am closer to thee than breathing, nearer than hands
and feet, and "I will never leave thee, nor forsake thee."
If you mount up to heaven, I will be there; if, temporarily, you make your bed in hell, I will be there. If you
walk through the valley of the shadow of death, I will be
there.*

*Do not fear—it is I! Do not fear—"I will never leave
thee, nor forsake thee." Do not fear! I am the source of
thy life; I am thy life; and I am closer to thee than breathing. I am in the midst of thee; I am in the center of thee.*

*Put your entire faith in Me—the I within your being.
Do not fear this external world of thing or thought, for
I in the midst of thee am the only power. I have given
dominion to thee through this that is at the center of
thy being.*[4]

And so again we shall hear:

[4] The italicized portions of this book are spontaneous meditations
which have come to the author during periods of uplifted consciousness
and are not in any sense intended to be used as affirmations, denials,
or formulas. They have been inserted in this book from time to time
to serve as examples of the free flowing of the Spirit. As the reader
practices the Presence, he, too, in his exalted moments, will receive ever
new and fresh inspirations as the outpouring of the Spirit.

*"The Lord thy God in the midst of thee is mighty.
. . . He performeth the thing that is appointed for me.
. . . The Lord will perfect that which concerneth me."*

Always there is that Source within us with which we are at-one, and if good is to come into our experience, it must come through the Source, through our own consciousness. We must abide in this realization and truth:

I am one with the Father, and all that the Father has is mine. The presence of God in me is my safety and security. He that is within me is greater than he that is in the world; He that is within me will go before me to make the crooked places straight; He that is within me will go to prepare mansions for me.

It is we who must consciously and specifically abide in this Word, day by day, until eventually we are abiding there every day, all the days. In other words, it becomes a matter of praying without ceasing, but without ever once asking God for anything. God is infinite intelligence and knows our needs; God is divine love and will never withhold anything; and therefore our prayers should never be an asking or telling God. Our prayers must always be an acknowledgment of God, an acknowledgment that He is closer to us than breathing, an acknowledgment that He is our eternal life, that He is the mind, intelligence, and wisdom of our being, that He is our bread and meat and wine.

Let us not seek outside ourselves for what we shall eat or drink, or wherewithal we shall be clothed! Work—yes!

Work is our destiny, because God is working out a destiny—a spiritual destiny—through us; and because our destiny is to be about our Father's business, we shall always have work to do. We shall always be busy, and the closer the contact we make with our Father, the busier we shall be and the more hours we shall work; but we will work as a means of expressing ourselves, and our supply will be the reflex action of that expression. It may come directly from our work, or it may not; but it will not concern us how it comes because we shall be living in the assurance that it does not have to come from the outside; it does not have to come from our labors, since it is our inheritance. From the beginning, "I and my Father are one," and all that is necessary to demonstrate this truth is to live in the Word.

The materialistic way of living places its emphasis on acquiring and achieving the things of this world. The spiritual way of living is a resting in the Word, and letting Love flow out—the love of God, the love of our neighbor, the love of truth, the love of life. Too much of our lives and too many of our prayers have been merely an attempt to increase the length of human life, the amount of human good, human supply, or human companionship, without ever giving a thought to what the kingdom of God is like. We call ourselves Christians, but we forget that the Master said, "My kingdom is not of this world." Therefore, it is futile to try to get more of what this world has.

The Master said, "My peace I give unto you: not as the world giveth, give I unto you," but *My* peace, *My* peace. And what is this *My* peace, this God-peace, this

Christ-peace? What is this kingdom of God like—not just the kingdom of a hundred per cent increase in income, not just the kingdom of a heart that beats normally or muscles that are strong? What is My kingdom like, My kingdom, which is not of this world? And what is this My peace, this peace which is not the peace the world can give by making us healthy or wealthy or famous? Just what is My peace?

It is a peace that flows out from within. It is a life, a prosperity, and a joy that flow out from us, but do not flow into us. It cannot be found out here; and yet, when it appears to us, it appears as a healthier body, a more comfortable and beautiful home, and a more satisfying companionship. Those things, however, are not the goal —they are merely the added things. The goal is finding My kingdom, the kingdom of God, and resting in My peace and My kingdom which are already established within us.

This is the great mystery: We embody within ourselves the whole kingdom of God—infinity, not just a little bit of the kingdom, not just a small portion of God, but the allness of God. "He that seeth me seeth him that sent me." The allness of God is embodied within us, infinity itself—eternality, immortality—but that infinity is a mystery until we learn to pray, learn to meditate, and then hear a Voice within us saying, "I in the midst of you am God."

CHAPTER II

ATTAINING THE GOD-EXPERIENCE

We must understand that the message of The Infinite Way is not to give the world a new teaching, but to give the world an experience. The Infinite Way is actually a God-experience, a Christ-experience. The Infinite Way is not its writings, lectures, or classes. These are the instruments *leading* us to The Infinite Way, but The Infinite Way itself is the God-experience.

It became very clear to a serious student one day, while meditating upon the subject of the desert and water, that talking about water or thinking about it would not quench his thirst. Not even seeing or touching water would satisfy. Only by drinking, and thus experiencing water, is thirst quenched. Almost from the beginning, I have realized that no matter *what* truth, or how *much* truth, we know, truth is not a healing agency. What we know of truth is merely a step leading to a certain state of consciousness, and that state of consciousness is the healing agency.

When one does not know the correct letter of truth, it is very difficult to acquire the spirit or consciousness which leads to the actual God-experience. So the earnest reading and study of the letter of truth are steps opening consciousness to a final experience; and when that experience takes place, harmonious living is quickly revealed and manifest.

It is essential that we understand the nature of God. Unless we know the nature of God, there is no way of knowing the nature of true prayer, because prayer is the avenue leading to God, and it is through prayer that we make our contact with God. It is through prayer and communion that we have the God-experience.

If we pray and our prayers are not answered, we can be assured, as James said, that it is because we have been praying amiss. If we have been praying, that is, knowing the truth, and have not arrived at the demonstration of harmony in our experience, we might just as well be honest with ourselves and admit, "I have been praying amiss; I have not been praying correctly; I have not known *how to pray*." If we make that admission, we shall be able to take the next step and say, "It is because I do not know God. If I knew God, I would know how to pray. Now, what *is* God?"

If we take into our meditation the question, "What is God?" ultimately we shall be led to the secret of prayer, and when we have achieved correct prayer, meditation, or communion, we shall be led to a God-experience, which is a "peace, be still" to any form of error that may ver touch us. As a matter of fact, continuing in the God-experience will prevent about ninety-odd per cent of the world's troubles ever touching us, and the little that may touch us will be quickly resolved.

Meditation is one of the very important teachings in the message of The Infinite Way, yet many people, even after a year or two of study, still do not know how to meditate. There are states and stages of meditation, just as there are states and stages of prayer and the healing consciousness. I would like now to give you a simple form of meditation, which in and of itself will lead to a higher sense of prayer than you have known before. Throughout the Writings you will find various illustrations of meditation. That is because the one given now may not be necessary a year from now, while another may be more suitable for you at a later time. Thus you progress from one state to another up to the highest form of meditation in which no thought enters.

The first step in meditation is to make yourself physically comfortable. Sit erect, with your spine straight, your feet planted firmly on the floor, your hands relaxed in your lap, and breathe normally. There is no mystical or occult reason for this; it is very simple: When the body is perfectly comfortable, one is not conscious of it. One can be, in a sense, "absent from the body, and . . . present with the Lord"—present with the Truth.

From there you go to the subject "What is God?" From your reading and study you have some concept of what God is, but that concept might easily be that of someone else. In this meditation you are not interested in another's concept of God; you are interested only in asking, "What is God?" and receiving the answer from God. The kingdom of God is within you, so the answer must come from *within your own being*.

After you have asked the question, assume a listening attitude as if you were waiting to hear the answer. While you wait, thoughts are bound to come, and you welcome them. These thoughts may be along the following lines but not necessarily so, because they will be individual with you. Quickly it will come to you that God is life, not merely because the Bible and the metaphysical books say so, but because it is already clear in your own mind that without life in the world there would be nothing. So if God is manifested in any way at all, it must be as life.

The moment that thought comes, you begin to think of the life of man—your life. If you are a parent, you think of how that life became the life of your child. Right there you begin to see, "Why, wait a minute. I couldn't have given life to that child. I don't know how to impart life. Now, how *did* life impart itself to my child?" You soon realize that there was an activity taking place within the mother, for which the mother was just a vehicle. You may have further thoughts along that line, and eventually you will realize that the trees are living, the flowers are living, the fish and the birds are living. We have just said that *God* is life. Then those things which we call trees, the song of the bird, and the fragrance of the flower are all God—God expressing Itself.

Expanding the meditation further, you see that a seed, until it is planted in the ground, cannot sprout—it remains a seed. Forever and forever it remains a seed until life, acting upon it, arouses the life within it. There again you see life, and that is God. God, permeating the elements of the earth and acting upon the seed, brings forth fruit after Its kind. You contemplate the universe—the light and warmth of the sun, the brilliance of the stars, the waxing and waning of the moon, the planets, the formation of clouds—and again you praise God: "They are living, living, living! God is life! 'The heavens declare the glory of God; and the firmament sheweth his handiwork.' All is God revealing Itself, God announcing Itself."

As you look about at the infinity of the forms of flowers, fruit, trees, foliage, the infinity of life in the universe, suddenly you realize the nature of prayer, and you will think, "Wait a minute. All these things exist without anyone's praying for them. These things exist as the activity of God, Itself, without any human intervention, petition, or affirmation. And I have been praying for these things—for supply, for beauty, for harmony—and here they are. They are God, Itself, not something separate and apart from God. They are Life, Itself, and they are already here."

Before long you will understand that prayer is the recognition that life already *is*, and that *God is that life* regardless of the form as which it appears, and that it does not have to be prayed for, either in the old sense of petition or in the new sense of affirmation. You begin to see that prayer is this silent meditating, pondering, and recognizing of God as the Source of all that is. Recognizing God to be the very life heard in the bird's song, the very life in the flower's fragrance, you begin to understand Omnipresence, and to understand that prayer is the recognition of the omnipresence of God as the life of every form.

In this meditation you may think of *nothing* but God as Life, but in some future meditation you will be struck by the fact that the birds and the fish are being fed; so also the flowers and the trees are being fed with rain, sunshine, and with the earth's substance, and then you say, "Why, God is love"—not because John said it in Scripture, but because it is self-evident that God not only is the life of the trees, the flowers, and the birds, but God is love, because God is feeding and sustaining them. God is not only creating, but He is also maintaining, sustaining, feeding, and protecting. You may spend hours in which you will see the nature of God as Love appearing in this visible universe.

Another day, in your meditation, will come the realization that when you plant a coconut you get a coconut tree, when you plant a papaya you get a papaya tree, when you plant a pineapple you get a pineapple, and then you will know that God is law. God is law, and there are no exceptions to God's law. White begets white; black begets black; and a combination of white and black begets a combination of white and black: This is a law. Then you will see that you need not protect anyone or anything because the law of God is the protection unto Its own creation. God is first the creator of all, and that makes all that is the very image and likeness of God; God is the maintainer, and God is the law unto Its own creation. This realization is a high and effective form of prayer.

Since God is the life of all, and God-life, being eternal and immortal, all that *is*, is eternal and immortal. God is love, maintaining and sustaining Its own creation. God is law, the law of eternality and immortality. God is the very law of health, harmony, wholeness, holiness, and perfection. You see, meditation is really prayer, and prayer is meditation. Just as one grain of sand does not constitute a beach, so you can see that I have touched only the surface of the subject of meditation. You can go on for a year, or two or three, with the same question, "What is God?" and in every meditation receive a different answer, and with each answer will come a new and higher concept of prayer.

Someday, while meditating and pondering this idea, "What is God?" realizing now the nature of prayer, you will suddenly find that you cannot think any more; you have come to the end of thought about God and prayer. Then you will sit there, quietly, at peace—no more thoughts, no more questions, no more answers, just peace. Thought will be quieted; the inner ear will open; and a long deep breath, like a sigh of relief or a sense of release, will probably come to you. It is as if you were escaping from something, as if a burden were dropping off your shoulders. Sometimes it is like a release of air from within the lungs, sometimes a short quick breath. It will appear in many different ways, and when that release or relief comes you will be so full of the Spirit that you will want to get right up and do the work that lies ahead for the day, or perhaps some work that has been neglected. With that release will come divine wisdom, divine guidance, and divine strength, for this reason:

That deep breath, that "click" or release, was a God-experience—the actual presence or activity of God in your consciousness. It may announce itself in some other way, but you will know it by your reaction: You are tingling; there is new life in you; there is an awareness that is more than your human selfhood; and you will know that it is the presence and the activity of God in you.

You will now understand Paul when he says, "I live; yet not I, but Christ liveth in me." You will have a feeling, an inner knowing, "This is the very Christ that I am experiencing. This is the presence and the Spirit of God. Through me, It does *all* things: It goes before me to make the crooked places straight; It goes ahead to prepare a place for me; It is the cement in human relationships, the love binding us together, the understanding between me and all those whom I meet; It is the guidance, the wisdom, and the strength for the task I must perform. It is the healing power."

Many spiritual students believe that if they can just change a sick body into a well body, unemployment into employment, a bad person into a good person, that is spiritual demonstration. Please believe me: These are *not* demonstrations. These are the *effects* of demonstration. The demonstration is that awareness of God's presence— the deep breath, the "click," or the sense of release—*that is the demonstration.* When you achieve that, health, employment, supply, home, companionship—whatever is necessary—automatically follow because these are the *added* things. In the message of The Infinite Way, you will find that we cannot demonstrate person, place, thing, or condition. We can demonstrate only the presence of God, the activity of God in us, the realization of God. When we have achieved *that* demonstration, all these *things* are added unto us.

If we were to believe, for one moment, that we have any way of demonstrating health or wealth for friends or students, we would mislead first ourselves and then them. We have no power to demonstrate health or supply for anyone, but we *can* demonstrate the presence of God. We *can* get very still within and, with patience, come to a state of consciousness where we *feel* the very living presence of God, where we feel the stir and the activity of God within, where we feel such a complete release from human fears that we know God is on the field. That is all we can do. From there on, it is that presence of God that makes whatever adjustment is necessary in the mind or body, the Spirit or Soul of friend or student, and brings about his release from discord, inharmony, or lack.

Our Master, Christ Jesus, said that he could not heal or feed. "I can of mine own self do nothing . . . the Father that dwelleth in me, he doeth the works," and I say to you that we cannot go beyond the demonstration of Christ Jesus. You will never be able to heal and feed the multitudes. You will be able to demonstrate only the presence, power, and activity of God in your own consciousness, and then It, the Father within you, will multiply the loaves and fishes, will heal the multitudes, and will even raise the dead. *It* will do that. Whenever you do any work of a spiritual nature—prayer, communion, or treatment—for yourself, your family, friends, or students, please remember this: You cannot heal anyone. You cannot feed, employ, or enrich anyone, so turn away from the claim. The claim may be John Jones or Mary Smith; the claim may be cancer or tuberculosis; it may be poverty, lack, limitation, or unhappiness. Whatever the claim may be, drop it, and realize there is only one thing you can do, and that is to gain the conscious awareness of the presence of God.

How do you achieve it? Oh, there are hundreds of ways. As a beginner, you sit down and just ponder, "What is God? What is prayer?" and then be still and wait for the answer to come; or at another time, "Father, I know that physical health is here today and gone tomorrow. A person may have a perfect heart today and die of heart disease next year; he may have perfect lungs today and tuberculosis next year. So I know that just having a perfect heart and lungs is not health. Now, Father, what is spiritual health?" Since there is no possible way for you even to think about that, you will quickly settle down into this peaceful atmosphere of listening, and when release comes you will have attained that awareness of God's presence.

Someone may come needing help on employment. You are not an employment agency, nor are you an employer, so there is nothing that you can do humanly or mentally about that problem. But you can sit quietly realizing, "Father, I can do nothing of myself, but as I attain the conscious awareness of Thy presence, harmony will be made evident." So you meditate. It makes no difference whether you meditate on "What is God? What is prayer? What is health? What is employment?" so long as you meditate on some divine idea until you come to the end of that particular subject. Then you will find yourself at peace.

Do not try to still the human mind or to stop thinking, because that is impossible. No one has ever succeeded in doing that, but as you meditate upon the subject you have chosen, the human mind of its own accord will become very still, very quiet. Should a few vagrant thoughts keep running around, do not be concerned; they will not interfere with the activity of God. Think about the spiritual idea as long as thoughts will come, and soon peace will descend upon you, and the answer will come. It may come in a Bible verse or as a spiritual truth. It may come as an inner assurance that all is well, or in a deep sense of peace and release. On the other hand, it may come in just a deep breath or "click." There will be no doubt about it, and you will forget the problem and forget the solution and go on about your business, until suddenly someone will call and tell you, "I have a wonderful job," or "I am feeling better," or "I am completely healed."

Sometimes, however, you will receive a call and the person says, "I don't feel any better. In fact, I'm feeling worse, so you had better pray again." When that happens, do not be disturbed. Just go back and pray again. If your friend calls back every day for a year, continue praying. There are good reasons why everyone does not receive an instantaneous healing—reasons that are good for the practitioner as well as for the patient.

When Jesus multiplied the loaves and fishes, he meant to show the *principle* of supply, but the Hebrews were unable to see that. They wanted only to be fed. You may have a student or friend, or even a member of your family who is interested, at the moment, only in the loaves and fishes—a healing. He may receive a healing, perhaps several, but the day will come when he himself must learn to demonstrate the presence and power of God in his own consciousness. Sometimes a *little* delay or sometimes a *long* delay is good and necessary to reveal that we do not go to God for loaves and fishes. We go to God for *God*, and when we have God, the loaves and fishes are added unto us.

How would you feel toward a so-called friend who was a friend only for what he could get from you? You would soon lose interest in that friendship. But what a joyous thing to *give* to a friend as long as he is not expecting you to give. So it is with God. How bountiful and wonderful God is when we love God for God, when we seek God for God, when all that we want in life is the attainment of the God-experience. The Psalmist says, "As the hart panteth after the water brooks, so panteth my soul after thee, O God. My soul thirsteth for God, for the living God." There must be but one goal when we meditate or pray, and that is to have a God-experience—*an awareness, a consciousness of the presence of God.*

Never, never try to heal or enrich anyone, but pray only for the realization that I and the Father are one, and when you have gained *that*, your patient, if at all receptive and responsive, will be healed.

The answer to the question, "Why isn't everyone healed, and healed more quickly?" lies in the Master's parable of the sower. When there is no depth of love for God, and no depth to the search for God, the seed does not take root. Of course, if these people keep coming back, they will develop a greater depth of fertility. The spiritual seed that falls into fertile soil will bring forth great fruitage. That does not mean that you should ever sit in judgment or condemnation, nor does it mean that you should refuse help to anyone, but it is an explanation of why you may work longer with some people than with others. Even barren soil will eventually take on some fertility if you will work with it patiently.

Do not indulge in self-criticism or judgment if your particular friend or student does not respond quickly. It is not your fault, it is not God's fault, nor is it the fault of the teaching. When a person follows a spiritual teaching with sincerity, with real integrity, and with the love of God in his heart, he will arrive at his goal. There is enough truth in any spiritual teaching to enable the student to reach his final goal, in proportion to his own integrity, loyalty, and fidelity to God. It is the misapplication of the terms *loyalty* and *fidelity*, in relation to a teacher, a teaching, or an organization, that sometimes leads one astray.

Everyone can reach, in this present life, a high degree of happiness, wholeness, and perfection, and if the soil is fertile he can attain the full degree of mystic, or Christhood, the divine spiritual sonship. Everyone can attain some measure, and a very good and harmonious measure, but be assured it will be in proportion as he understands that the *object and intent* of meditation, prayer, or communion is the God-experience.

So whenever you sit down to give help to a person or to cats, dogs, birds, or plants, just forget them and say,

"All I seek, Father, is a realization of Thy presence."
Then meditate or pray in any of the ways that have been
shown forth, and each meditation will lead to the final
step where you do not pray at all—where you just wait
and let a sense of peace enfold you, culminating in release. That release itself is the Presence that goes before
you to make the crooked places straight.

CHAPTER III

GOD IS

Prayer is our contact with God, the infinite Source of our being, of which we can have no actual intellectual knowledge, and for which we have used such terms as Mind, Life, Truth, Love, Spirit, the Infinite Invisible. God is the *only* creative principle of the universe, the creative principle of all that *is;* and since this creative Principle operates from the standpoint of supreme intelligence, without beginning and without end, it becomes necessary to know how to make *contact* or to become *one* with It. Unless we learn the way, we cannot avail ourselves of the omnipresence, omnipotence, and omniscience of God.

Prayer, sometimes called communion, is the avenue through which we make our contact, find our oneness, or *realize* God. Prayer is the means of bringing into our individual experience the activity, the law, the substance,

47

the supply, the harmony, and the *allness* of that which we call God. This is one of the most important points for all students of spiritual wisdom to know, to understand, to practice, and to live.

In understanding the infinite nature of God, we understand the infinite nature of our *own being*. "I and my Father are one" *assures* the infinite nature of your being and my being. This fact is not dependent upon one's being a student of truth, but is dependent solely upon one's relationship to God, and that relationship is oneness—*oneness*. We shall hear much more about that word *oneness* as we progress.

We must accept anything that is spiritually true of any individual, saint or sinner, as being true of you and of me, since the relationship of God to Its creation is a universal one. When the Master taught that I and the Father are one, he was very careful to assure us that he spoke of *your* Father and *my* Father. He was revealing a universal spiritual truth. What, then, separated the demonstration of Christ Jesus from that of the Hebrew rabbis of his day? Or, what separated the demonstration of the Master from that of his students and his disciples? The relationship was the same, "I and my Father are one"— your Father and my Father. We are all *one* in this relationship in Christ Jesus, in truth, in spiritual reality, so the difference in demonstration is the difference in *realization*.

The Master realized his true identity. He recognized his relationship with the Father, with God, as the source of his being. He recognized God as his life—bread, wine, water. He therefore recognized his substance or supply as infinite, his life as eternal, his health as perfect. Since all these had their source in the Father, they were his by divine inheritance; they revealed the right, the privilege, and the experience of the Father-Son relationship: "Son, thou art ever with me, and all that I have is thine." The Master, in his complete recognition of this, was able to demonstrate it. The disciples, not quite so sure, not quite so deep in the realization, demonstrated a measure of healing power and supply, though not in the same degree as the Master, and the only reason for the difference in degree of demonstration was the difference in the degree of realization.

The fact that you are hearing with your ears and seeing with your eyes is not prayer and will not make your demonstration; but if something deep within your heart, a comforting assurance within your consciousness, responds with "Yes! This is the truth. I know that only in the realization of this, am I one with the Father," this is the degree of your realization of the nature of prayer. Prayer is this assurance of truth within you. Prayer is never going to God for something. Prayer is never a desire for something, unless it may be your desire to know God or the desire to become more keenly aware of God's presence. Many students, so steeped either in old theology or in modern metaphysics, lapse into a belief that they can go to God for something—health, supply, employment, companionship, or healing—and thereby postpone their demonstration of harmony.

It will do no good to take thought for your life, your health, or your supply; it will do no good to go to God with a request, a petition, or a desire, because God possesses nothing that He is withholding, and God is withholding nothing that He possesses. God is infinite active being. All that God *is* and all that God *has* is flowing constantly into manifestation, expression, and form, and to think that prayer will influence God to speed it up, or to deliver it to your doorstep, is foolishness.

Harmony quickly becomes your experience when you can agree that there is no use in going to God for anything. Please remember that when I say "agree" I speak of *feeling* an assurance or agreement within, a deep conviction within, not just mouthing, "Yes, I believe. I agree with the Master. I am a Christian and I accept his teaching." That amounts to less than nothing. Can you *feel* the rightness of this? Can you *feel* the truth of the Master's tremendous revelation that "your Father knoweth that ye have need of these things. . . . for it is your Father's good pleasure to *give* you the kingdom"? If you cannot feel this, for a long, long while to come, do not go to God for anything. Work within yourself; pray within your own being; commune within until you *do* come to a feeling, an awareness, or an agreement that the Master really *knew* that the Father knows that you have need of these things, and it is His good pleasure to *give* you the kingdom long before you ask.

Prayer is a recognition of this truth of God's love for His own creation; it is the inner *knowing* that the Father has *never* forsaken His creation. As we look out at the world and see all the disease, sin, death, and calamity, we are apt to question this, but in so doing we are forgetting the wisdom of John when he admonishes us, "Judge not according to the appearance, but judge righteous judgment."

We have been seeing with our eyes and hearing with our ears, when we should have been seeing with our inner eyes, hearing with our inner ears, with that spiritual awareness that judges not by appearances, but judges spiritual judgment. Then we will know that all of the sin, disease, death, lack, limitation, and chaos in the world today come for only one reason, and that they come only to those who are living through material sense; to those still desiring and wanting to get, to acquire, and to achieve; to those who, as yet, do not know the infinite nature of their own being and the fact that, because of this infinite nature, they must let it *pour out from them* instead of trying to make it add more *to* them.

The commonly accepted prayer, both orthodox and metaphysical, must fail, because it is an attempt, in most cases, to add something, achieve something, accomplish something, or receive something; whereas the infinite nature of your own being as one with God means that your "vessel" is already full. All that the Father has is already yours. Can more be added? The great poet, Browning, gave us a beautiful secret when he wrote, "Truth is within ourselves . . . and to know . . . consists in opening out a way whence the imprisoned splendor may escape. . . ."

In judging by appearances, we come upon a phase of belief which causes the entire trouble and inharmony of human existence: the judgment of good and evil. This, we say, is good and *this* is evil. Of course, the very thing we are calling good today may, by a change of tradition or society, be evil tomorrow, and some of those things that are very evil today may be commonplace, normal, and natural tomorrow. But we are not thinking of that at this moment when we judge by appearances. We are judging by the present standards of society or the present traditions that have been handed down to us, and instantly we label a thing good or evil, basing our judgment entirely upon human opinion, human belief, and human theory. As long as we are looking out upon the world through human eyes, we will always be seeing that which is good and that which is evil, even though the classifications change with each generation.

In order rightly to understanding the subject of prayer, we must, this instant, give up our human judgment as to good or evil. No longer can we gratify our sense of psychological wisdom by judging those of our family, business, or community circles, but we must relinquish and withdraw our opinions of good or evil, intelligent or stupid, honest or dishonest, moral or immoral, and look at each individual with no condemnation, no criticism, and with no judgment, but only with the realization that God *is*.

God *is*; Life *is*. We are permitted no further judgment. *God is*. It is a matter of training oneself to form no opinion whatsoever. It is so easy and satisfying to one's ego to be a good judge of human nature, to be able humanly to evaluate those whom we meet, and of course humanly we may be right; but looking out at the world and judging mankind, putting labels on people, and abiding by those human opinions and decisions will only lead to trouble. There is but one way to come out from among them and be separate, and that is in our agreement that God made all that was made, and all that God made is good; in our agreement that God, Spirit, is the life, the Soul, and the mind of individual being. How can we possibly accept a teaching which reveals God as the Life of all being, as the creative Principle of all being, and then designate some good and some bad?

The woman taken in adultery was not labeled by the Master. "Woman, where are those thine accusers? . . . Neither do I condemn thee." To the thief on the cross, he said, "Today shalt thou be with me in paradise," and to the man born blind, "Neither hath this man sinned, nor his parents." Do you begin to understand the necessity of foregoing all censure, all condemnation that is based on appearances? Every spiritual teaching and revelation from 1500 b.c. is based upon the postulates "Love thy neighbor as thyself" and "Do unto others as you would have others do unto you." Prayer is our contact with God, and we have no contact with God unless we love our neighbor as ourselves.

This will, of course, deprive us of many of our social and political discussions, for we will no longer be able to blame our families or friends, our business associates, or the heads of our government for our troubles, circumstances, and depressions. This calls for discipline on the part of each one of us, and it calls for something more: It calls for a deep and great love of God. No one can come into the holy atmosphere of God voicing criticism, judgment, or condemnation of his fellow man. "Therefore if thou bring thy gift to the altar, and there rememberest that thy brother hath aught against thee; leave there thy gift before the altar, and go thy way; first be reconciled to thy brother, and then come and offer thy gift."

There can be no spiritual demonstration while we hold to human opinions of good and evil. When we look at the world with no opinions, judgments, or labels—not even good ones—but with the realization that God is, we set up a sort of a vacuum within. Into that vacuum surges the spiritual wisdom defining and evaluating that which is before us, and this we find to be entirely different from our human estimate. Into our consciousness there comes a warmth, a feeling of love for mankind, and the realization that God is the allness of being. As one beholds this revelation of spiritual truth, he becomes ready for the next step—the step that makes him a healer, a savior, a reformer, a supplier in the universe.

Now the time comes when we must look at every condition—be it imprisonment in a prison, imprisonment in a sick body, imprisonment in lack or limitation—and withdraw the opinion of good or evil. We must be able to look at every situation and circumstance with the realization that God is. As I have said elsewhere in my writings, it takes a high degree of spiritual consciousness to look a serious disease in the face and behold the Christ. This does not mean that we are to look at sin, disease, poverty, and imprisonment, and call them good. This does not mean that we are to make affirmations and say that they are spiritual and harmonious, nor does it mean to call them evil and desire to rise above them or to improve or heal them. No, no, no. Withholding all human judgment, realize only *God is, God alone is.*

At this point you may ask, "What is the *principle* involved?" In acknowledging God as infinite, can you acknowledge a sick or sinful person, a sinful or diseased condition? Can you accept any person or condition as requiring healing, changing, or improving? No, you cannot. What happens when you witness what human sense would call error or label as error and you pray for its removal? There is only one answer to that—failure.

Remember, you are not called upon to look at erroneous persons or conditions and call them good or spiritual, or to say that an erroneous person is the Son of God. An erroneous person is *not* the Son of God. You are asked to give up all opinion, theory, or belief, and to withhold all judgment. Do not declare anyone or anything good. "Why callest thou me good? there is none good but one, that is, God."

Call no one good and no condition good, but also call no one evil and call no condition evil. Learn to look at every person and every situation with just two words, *God is,* or *It is. Is—is—is:* not will be, not to be healed, improved, or removed. *God is. Harmony is. It is! It is now!* In the realization that *God is,* will be revealed all spiritual entity and perfection. You will not then see human evil turned to goodness; you will not see human poverty turned to riches; you will not see human disease turned to human health; you will not see human guilt turned to human virtue; *but you will perceive the Spirit of God!* You will perceive the activity and law of God right where there had seemed to be a good or bad person, or a good or bad condition.

The chapter entitled "The New Horizon" in my book *The Infinite Way* makes it clear that we are not seeking to change bad humanhood into good humanhood. The object of our work and study is the attaining of that mind which was in Christ Jesus—that is, attaining that same state of spiritual consciousness, or some degree of it, that was in Christ Jesus, so that we may behold the spiritual world, the spiritual man, the Son of God. "My kingdom is not of this world." The kingdom of God is a spiritual kingdom, a spiritual universe, governed by spiritual law. It is a spiritual *substance* that never began and will never end.

We can better understand this if we stop to think that there has never been a time when two times two was not four. There has never been a time when a rose seed would produce anything other than a rose, or a pineapple seed produce anything other than a pineapple. The law of "like begets like" has been in effect since before time began. It has been, it is, and it ever will be. Praying in the ordinary sense of prayer will not bring it about. All good already *is*.

Even in the depth of so-called depressions, the land brought forth bountiful crops, the oceans were teeming with fish, and birds filled the skies. God had no power to increase His supply. It was *already* infinite. It was more than the earth could use. It still is, regardless of the seeming lack and high prices, for which ignorance is the only excuse. The world is producing more than it can consume and use. Would prayer to God for increased supply actually increase the amount of good or products? No, there is already a sufficiency for everyone.

The question naturally arises, "How do we avail ourselves of this sufficiency?" and the answer is, "Through
prayer." And what is prayer? Prayer is this feeling, this
conviction, this knowing within that these words are true.
God is. Would you change that? Would you change *anything* that God has made? Would you ask for improve-
ment in God's universe? Would you ask God to let you
influence the laws, the substance, and the activity of
God's own creation? "Yea, though I walk through the
valley of the shadow of death, I will fear no evil: for
thou art with me." *God is*. Can there be more than that
to pray for? The feeling of the rightness of that statement, *"God is,"* is your prayer. Right now, it would be
enough if you could drop all desires, all wishes, even all
hopes, and in time this feeling, or realization, will lead
you into deeper and deeper planes of consciousness and
into deeper realms of prayer. *God is*. Is that not enough?

Again I say to you, do not judge by appearances. Look
at every person, every thing, every situation, every condition, with just the realization that *God is*, and then *let*
the spiritual reality be made visible to you by the Father
within.

CHAPTER IV

GOD IS ONE

Hear, O Israel: The Lord our God is one Lord.

DEUTERONOMY 6:4

In our agreement and understanding that God is one, God has no opposite, and there is no opposition. With God as one, there is only one activity, one being, one cause, one power, one law.

When the Master was asked which of the commandments was the greatest, he answered, "Thou shalt love the Lord thy God with all thy heart, and with all thy soul, and with all thy mind." Therefore, the first and greatest commandment is, "Thou shalt have none other gods before me." We think of God as power, and so the commandment is: Thou shalt acknowledge no other power but God. What, then, are we fearing—germs, infection, contagion? Since God is the only power, can these things have any power? According to the Master's teaching, they could have no power except such as was given them by God.

Do we fear lack or limitation? How can lack or limitation affect us? Do we fear wars and hydrogen bombs? According to the first commandment, *only God is power.* What would happen to the power of the hydrogen bomb *if* we could realize God as the only power? Think on this deeply, because there must come a moment of transition when we can intellectually declare, "Why, that is right. *If* God *is* the only power, what have we to fear from all the so-called powers of earth and hell?" Then there must come a moment of transition when we go from that intellectual agreement to spiritual agreement, a *feeling* of agreement within, "Yes, that *is* the truth; I *feel* the truth of that *one* power."

"Thou shalt have none other gods before me"—therefore, God is the only law. We are now faced with a startling question: Is there a law of disease? *God is the only law.* What, then, is causing disease? What is perpetuating it, if there is no law of disease? We are told in Scripture, "According to your faith be it unto you"; and therefore, if you have confidence, faith, or belief that there is a law of disease, so it must be unto you. You see, the world is trying to remove disease through the study of the *laws* of disease, and there are no such laws.

According to the Master's teaching and the teaching of all spiritual wisdom throughout the ages, there is only *one* power, *one* law, *one* being. Think, now, because this is the point to which we are leading: There is nothing in all this world to use God-power for or against. Since there is no *power* apart from God, there is no sin, no evil; since there is no *law* apart from God, there is no law of disease, no law of lack or limitation, and we no longer have to turn to God to overcome these things, to help us rise above them, to destroy, correct, or remove them.

That is the function of this teaching, the teaching which we may call a teaching of *is*—just the two letters *i-s*, *is*—and it is just as simple as the revelation which brought The Infinite Way into existence, also a two-letter word *a-s*, *as*. God is expressed, manifest, *as* you and *as* me; God is appearing *as* your being and my being; God is appearing *as*, God manifest *as*, this universe. There is no selfhood apart from God since God appears as this universe; there is no condition apart from God since God appears *as* the substance and activity of this universe. God appearing *as*, logically leads up to God *is*. *Is* has no point of comparison, since it always, eternally and immortally, is what it *is*, and that *is*, is Spirit. It is not some degree of human good, nor is it some degree of human evil. *It is*—spiritually, harmoniously, joyously, eternally, immortally, infinitely *is*. *Is*.

Law *is*. There is not good law or bad law. There is only law—God *is*. There is not good or strong power, not good or evil power: There is only power—God *is*. There is no power to oppose anything, so there is no use praying to it to overcome our enemies, no use praying to it to overcome sin or sinful desires or appetites, no use praying to it to overcome disease, since there is only one power and the power that is, *is* God.

We must be arriving, now, at a state of consciousness called *is*, and we must rest in that *is*. We have no evil to oppose or from which to be protected, and we do not have to pray in order to get God to do something for us, since God, Good, already *is*. If, deep within us, we can feel a responsive agreement, that is our prayer, our treatment, and our communion with God. "Hear, O Israel: The Lord our God is one Lord"—one in essence, one in cause, one in effect, one infinite Good.

You are led into a continuing state of consciousness in which you do not, even by suggestion, think of turning to God to do something for you, since that of which you are thinking already *is*. Never do you pray for something or someone. Your whole prayer becomes an inner agreement that it already *is* and always has been. "Before Abraham was, I am. . . . lo, I am with you alway, even unto the end of the world. . . . I will never leave thee, nor forsake thee." *Is, am, is*—I *am* with you; it *is* so. No longer do you reach mentally for some statement of truth: There is now only one statement of truth, and it comes in one word, *is*. It already *is*.

Many, many years ago it was revealed to me, "That which I am seeking, I *am*. I already *am*; it already *is*; it always *is*." With that understanding came the realization that I could give up seeking; I could give up searching; I could even give up praying. *It already is.* And now my prayer is no longer asking or affirming: My prayer is the realization, the recognition, of *is*.

Whatever of good has come into your consciousness in the form of desire or hope *already is*. There is no power to bring it to you tomorrow. The question of time enters here. You cannot live yesterday, can you? No good can come into your experience yesterday, and so far as we know, no one has ever lived tomorrow. The spiritual literature of the world seems very much in accord that *now* is the only time we live, that *now* is the only time we will live, and for that reason, *now* is the only time.

So you can see, prayer that would have to do with yes‧ terday or last year, or perhaps the last incarnation, would be a waste of time. You will never live an hour ago, so there is no use praying for, or about, anything that concerns itself with an hour ago. "Let the dead bury their dead." Let yesterday bury yesterday, and let us concern ourselves with *now*. Since we cannot live tomorrow there is no reason to wish or to desire or to hope for tomorrow. There is only one time in which our prayers can materialize, and that time is *now*.

It is for this reason that we must learn and understand the instantaneousness and the spontaneousness of healing and reformation, since it can take place only *now*. What great fact do we discover? Above all, we discover that *I am! I am now!* You will ask, "What is *I am?*" That, you must learn from within, but one thing is certain: *If I am,* all that the Father is, and all that the Father has, *is* right now in that *I am-ness.* All that the Father has *is now.* All that the Father has *is mine now.* All that the Father is, *I am, now.* If you are able to follow this, you are feeling, "Why, that is just *is* again; *is*—not to be hoped for and not to be prayed for. Why not? Because in this *now* there is only one power, the one presence, the one law, which *I am.* All that God is, *I am now!"*

So far as we know, the Master never prayed for anything for himself. Can you understand why he never seemed to have a need? If it came to healing, he could heal multitudes; if it came to supply, he could take care of multitudes. At no point was he seeking to get or to acquire. The Bible states that he was an hungered, that he was tempted to turn the stones into bread. Was he tempted to believe in lack? No. He recognized his fulfillment, he recognized his divine sonship, he recognized that all that the Father had, was his *now*, and that he did not have to make it so. It already *is*. "Get thee behind me, Satan." Get behind me—the temptation to believe that I can acquire something a minute from now, when in this *now*-ness is my *is*-ness. It is now. I am. All that God is, I am.

Surely, deep within your consciousness comes the *feeling of agreement* that right now *I* am in the midst of you; all that ever has been is now; all that ever will be is now, for *now* is the only time—the divine harmony of God is your being now, and that is your prayer.

So, once again we are admonished to withhold all judgment, because if we judge by appearances the world is full of skies that sit on mountains, or car tracks that come together. Yet these are only appearances or illusions, only temptations to keep us from venturing forth.

You can readily see that you cannot discuss this with friends or relatives because they live by appearances, and appearances are the very bread and butter of their daily living. All of the conversation of humanhood is about appearances, so it is useless trying to talk, argue, or reason this out with them. Be still and know, but be very still. *Be very still* and spiritually know that this is the truth: There is no law of disease; there is no evil; there is no power that can harm. Spiritually feel the rightness of this. If you feel it spiritually, you are praying aright rather than praying amiss. If you can *feel* the rightness of the one law, the one presence, the one power—that there is nothing to overcome, nothing to destroy or to remove—then you will know, "I already am. It is; God is; harmony is."

As we walk through the experiences of each day, temptations to judge as to good or bad, sick or well, rich or poor, sin or purity will continually arise. We are faced, not only with the Master's three temptations, but with three million. There is always the temptation to look at the woman taken in adultery and throw a few stones, or at the thief caught in the act and judge. From morning to night we are tempted to believe in appearances and to label them good or bad, right or wrong, but we must resist these temptations by learning to look at person, circumstance, condition, or disease, and withhold judgment. We must realize *is*—*is*—and let the Father define, outline, and show forth that which spiritually *is*. "My kingdom is not of this world." There is no use trying to judge the spiritual kingdom from appearances—it will not work.

The study and practice of The Infinite Way is the development of spiritual consciousness. It is not going through human existence picking out all the wrong things and finding a system whereby to make them right. It is looking *through* the appearance of both human good and human evil, and learning to behold the spiritual reality which *is*, even where the appearance seems to be.

About 500 B.C. Lao-Tse stated, "A name cannot name the eternal. Nameless, it is the source of Heaven and Earth; with names one comes to creation and things." In other words, if you can name God, it is not God. And so it is that anything that you could think about God would represent only your *concept* of God. If you say, "God is love," that is a concept of God; it is not God. So praying to Love or to Mind would be praying to concepts, not to God. You could go through all the synonyms for God, and declare that God is this or that, and you would be wrong. That would not be God at all; it would be only a concept of God, and praying to it would bring no results. Since any thought that you might think about God would represent an opinion, a theory, or a concept and would not be God, how then are we in The Infinite Way to consider God? Actually, there is only one thing that you can know about God—*God is*. Of that you can be very sure.

You have no way of knowing whether God is mind, or God is life, or God is love. These may be quotations which merely represent ideas formulated by the saints, seers, and sages down through the ages. They may be perfectly correct in their estimate of what God is, but you will have to admit that anything that may be said about God represents a theory, a belief, an opinion, or a concept—all except one thing: *God is*. That you know— *God is*. "In all thy ways acknowledge him, and he shall direct thy paths. . . . Thou wilt keep him in perfect peace, whose mind is stayed on thee." Acknowledge Him and keep your mind stayed on the God that *is*. *God is*. That is enough to know. What more can you do in the way of communion with God than this inner acknowledgment that God is? All else may be speculation or opinion, but one thing which no man can take from you is the realization that God is. As long as you acknowledge that God is and rest in that inner assurance, in some way, mysterious to human sense, God will reveal all that you need to know about God.

We have been leading up to this very important point: Do not be concerned with what anyone *teaches* about the nature of God, and do not be concerned with what anyone has *written* about God. Much that you read and study may appear to be right to you; much you may question. There is only *one* fact about which you can feel complete agreement, about which no doubt will ever enter your thought: *God is.* Be satisfied with that until God reveals to you, from within your own being, *what* God is, *when* God is, *how* God is. Let God reveal Itself to you.

I have had my own inner experience with God, with the realization of God, and with the actual *feeling* of the presence of God, but I cannot make this real to you. Many could not even believe that I have had the experience. Unless you have had some measure of God-experience, how could you possibly know if I am telling the truth, or whether I, myself, might not be mistaken? I *know*, but I cannot convey that knowledge to you. On one point you are already in agreement—God is. If you willingly accept that *is*-ness of God, that inner point of awareness and realization that God *is*, and ponder it, soon God will define Itself. God will reveal Itself, unfold and disclose Itself within you, in an original way, and with each experience will come some measure of what we call healing.

You will not find health and wealth added to you; you will find that health and wealth have been included in you since before even Abraham was. You will find that since God is the infinite nature of your being, all harmony and all good are included in the infinitude of that one spiritual Being.

This you will experience for yourself, not by believing me and not by accepting my word. I only wish that, by believing me, spiritual wisdom and demonstration could come to you, but it cannot be so. Spiritual experience can come only through your own realization. I can tell you only this: If you, without prejudice or opinion, without a theory or concept of what God is, can realize, "God is, that I know," and dwell with that and ponder it, keeping your thought in that line, from out of the depths of your consciousness within will come the experience revealing what God is, and how God operates and acts throughout this marvelous universe. This will be through spiritual discernment, and this will not come merely by agreeing with what others have said or written about God. Spiritual discernment will come with every God-experience, and you can have a God-experience only through knowing the truth. And what is the only truth that you know? God is—that is all the spiritual wisdom you know or will know until God reveals more from within your own being.

The ancient Hebrews said, "The Lord our God is one Lord," but that is also a restatement of a concept of God. We go on from there and say that God is one power, one law, but until God, Itself, reveals that, it remains a concept. To me, it is no longer a concept—it is a revealed truth because of an experience that took place in my consciousness, but to you it may be just a statement that I am repeating. One thing you do know—*God is*. Hold that to yourself, live with it, be satisfied with it until, to what you already *know*, to what you already *have* of spiritual wisdom, will be added the balance, "For whosoever hath, to him shall be given, and he shall have more abundance." You *have* this spiritual wisdom that *God is*, and by pondering it, meditating upon it, and thinking upon it within your own being, there will be added unto you all the rest: *who* God is; *what* God is; *how* God is. The way will be made clear to you from within your own being.

I have but one wish for the students of The Infinite Way, and all others on the Path, and that is, not that they accept what *my* experience in and with God has been, but that each one may himself experience God, know God, feel God, love and understand God, and finally realize Godhood.

CHAPTER V

GOD AS LAW IN OPERATION

Probably the idea that we like best of all to entertain is the idea of God as Love. About four hundred years before the birth of Jesus, Socrates recognized that God's love is known by His law. At some time on our spiritual journey, it becomes necessary to ponder the idea of God as Law, and in so doing we discover that we must give great attention to that idea if we are to bring our lives into harmony, wholeness, and completeness—into oneness, or at-one-ment, with Truth, with Love.

The science of electricity is governed by the law of electricity, and one does not set up an electrical wiring system without first knowing that law, because any violation of that law will result in someone's being hurt.

How true also is the law which is God. Many, many people are trying to live without bringing their lives into harmony with God's law, and the results are sad indeed.

Disregard of the law of God causes suffering from sin, disease, discord, and inharmony. Because of religious teachings which have almost entirely dropped the revelation and unfoldment of God as law, most people actually believe they can live their own lives in the way they want to live them, as long as they are careful not to violate or to get caught violating legal law. They do not realize that there is a law in operation much greater and more powerful than any law ever written into the statutes of any nation.

I was thinking of this recently in connection with forgiveness. An occasion arose in which forgiveness was almost out of the question, and regardless of all the unfoldment and understanding that had been given through the writings of The Infinite Way, there seemed to be no way to bring forgiveness into this situation. Then I thought of a certain man who, seemingly through no fault of his own, had suffered a very sad fate. As far as the public was concerned, a great wrong, a great evil, had been committed, of which he was the victim and for which he was not responsible. The thought came to me, "How do we know what was happening in the consciousness of the individual who was the victim? How do we know what he was attracting to himself? What was going on in his mind to attract such an experience to him?"

That set off a whole train of thought. The Master, who, we believe, knew the entire secret of the relationship existing between God and man, also knew that the way to bring about harmony in man's existence was through understanding the law of God. The Apostle Paul clearly states, "Be not deceived; God is not mocked: for whatsoever a man soweth, that shall he also reap." That is a strong saying, and a harsh one. If some of the things we have reaped in our experience were actually the reaping of what we ourselves have sown, then we are being called upon for a complete reorganization of our lives, our state of thought, and our state of consciousness. I am sure that very few of us consciously believe that the serious inharmonies and discords that have come into our experience are actually the result of our own sowing. Most of us are more inclined to believe that we are the innocent victims of other people's injustice and unkindness.

Paul, going further, shows us how to improve our sowing, so that our reaping will become more in accord with harmony. "For he that soweth to his flesh shall of the flesh reap corruption; but he that soweth to the Spirit shall of the Spirit reap life everlasting." At this point we, in The Infinite Way, thoroughly disagree with the metaphysical teaching that specific wrong thinking and specific wrong acts produce specific evils, diseases, or discords in our experience. Paul shows us that because God is Spirit, the laws of God are spiritual. If we have been accepting and entertaining material law as our basis of life, we are sowing to the flesh—to matter, materiality—and we are bound to reap finiteness, limitation, and inharmony.

This is a point of tremendous importance to those of us who are students on the Way. Probably every one of us has, in a measure, believed that some of our inharmonies and discords are due to other people, and right here is where we must bring the law of forgiveness into the picture. The first thing we ask is, "How can I ever forgive so-and-so for this terrible wrong?" We must forget about forgiving so-and-so, and we must acknowledge that as we have sown, so are we reaping. Instead of blaming another, we must make the acknowledgment, here and now, that some false state of being, some false state of thought or act within our own being, has drawn this experience to us, and had it not come through that particular individual, it most certainly would have come through some other, since the experience *had* to come to us. We drew it unto ourselves.

In holding someone in condemnation, you are sowing to the flesh and you will reap corruption, but in *not* blaming another you withdraw from that sowing. *Now* acknowledge that no one on earth, in heaven, or in hell, has the power to restrict, harm, or influence you in any way. *Now* acknowledge that all power resides within your Soul, and you will again be sowing to the Spirit and you will reap freedom, peace, and harmony.

Please understand that you are not being given a teaching of examining your thought to see what error you thought today or yesterday, or ten years ago, and correcting it. On the contrary, this is a teaching in which you acknowledge that material thinking must produce material conditions, but spiritual awareness—abiding in the spiritual Word—and letting the Word "abide in you," will produce spiritual fruitage. You can forget all of the past erroneous, even sinful, thinking, and begin afresh at any given point to wipe out the discords and inharmonies due to accepting or having accepted materiality. By turning to the Spirit, you begin at once to reap harmony, health, wholeness, and completeness.

"For he that soweth to his flesh shall of the flesh reap corruption" means that if you are placing your hope, faith, and confidence in form or in creation, you are sowing to the flesh; whereas, if you are placing your hope, faith, and reliance on the Spirit, on the Cause, on the Infinite Invisible, you are sowing to the Spirit. If you are under the belief that dollars or investments, crops or real estate, positions or payrolls, constitute supply, you are sowing to the flesh. You are putting your faith in some form of creation, and in sowing in that way you ultimately reap the loss, limitation, or valuelessness of those dollars, or the insecurity of those investments. Sooner or later you find that that in which you placed your reliance does not stand up.

It is the same if we place our faith in people. Scripture tells us, "Put not your trust in princes," and "Cease ye from man, whose breath is in his nostrils: for wherein is he to be accounted of?" If we place our faith in men, women, governments, or organizations, we will reap the sorrows and disappointments that come from having trusted "man, whose breath is in his nostrils"; whereas, if our complete reliance is on the Infinite Invisible, the governing Spirit, we will find ourselves being governed harmoniously in the outer picture. We must always have trustworthy and reliable men in positions of responsibility, but instead of *looking to them* for integrity, loyalty, and fidelity, we must look to *the Spirit that animates them*, and all men, to perform Its functions.

If we look to man for mercy, for justice, or for appreciation, sooner or later someone will fail us. In my booklet, *Love and Gratitude*, this entire principle is explained and becomes practical insofar as we are made to realize that our supply, even though it seems to come *through* people, is actually coming *from* the Infinite Invisible of our own being, the kingdom of God within us. If, even while accepting our supply from employers or investments, our love from husband, wife, children, or friends, we reserve a place within our consciousness for the realization, "Ah, yes, but my *dependence* isn't out there, since I know that the kingdom of God is within me, and *it* is the source of my supply and love," then we are sowing to the Spirit, and we will reap our spiritual supply even though the normal channels might be cut off. By sowing to the Spirit, we will reap spiritually, and our income and supply will continue, even though it may have to come through some other avenue. If, instead of looking to "man, whose breath is in his nostrils" for justice, co-operation, reward, and appreciation, we reserve, somewhere within us, one little corner for the recognition, "Ah, yes, I receive my recognition, my reward, my appreciation, and my gratitude from God, from the depth of the Soul within my being"—then we *let* it come *through* whomever it will.

Appreciation, reward, gratitude, love, and supply will never be withheld, and should those who may be the present means of these be removed, their places will be taken by others. As we sow spiritually, as we reserve this little area of our consciousness for the constant recognition that all appreciation, gratitude, and love are in the kingdom of God within us, we reap our spiritual good.

We have all been innocent victims of the calendar, because we have really believed that as each day and each year are crossed off we have grown older, and that the body has lost some of its strength, vitality, and keenness. We have believed that up to the thirties we gain in maturity, strength, and vitality, but after the thirties and forties we have accepted the universal belief that with the passing of years there is also the passing of youth, vitality, and strength. This is also a sowing to the flesh, because we put the harmony of our body and health where it is not. The power of our body and health, the power of our immortality is in the Spirit.

When once we realize that this infinite Spirit, or Soul, really governs and controls our physical and mental capacities, we shall never lose them: They will be maintained unto eternity. There will be no such thing as a body or mind wearing out at threescore years and ten, or at threescore years and fifty. We wear out through acceptance of the belief that the power of life, health, and strength is in the body. Once we understand that our physical, mental, and moral faculties are really activities of the Soul and that the body is just the instrument the Soul uses, the body will be as immortal as the Soul, as youthful, as vital, and as healthful as the Soul.

Forgiveness is also a law of God. The Master made it very clear that we were to forgive even our enemies, those who hate us and persecute us, those who despitefully use us, and if necessary we were to forgive them seventy times seven! Here is a law of God which every one of us has been violating. We have not forgiven our enemies, and certainly we have not forgiven seventy times seven. Forgiveness is one of the important laws mentioned so frequently in the Master's teaching.

Every one of us is entertaining a belief—perhaps just

a tiny belief—that some discord, some inharmony, some error in our experience, is due to someone else, either in the present, the past, or possibly in the future, and so we have violated the law of forgiveness. We cannot violate the law of God without suffering for it! We can violate human laws, legal and material laws, sometimes without repercussions, but there is no such thing as violating a spiritual law with impunity.

"Thou shalt love thy neighbor as thyself" is another law of God. As we think of our experiences of the past and the present, we shall find that there are many, many ways in which a greater love for our neighbor, considering the larger and more spiritual aspect of the word "neighbor," could flow out from us. This may not be entirely on the human level of love, but it may give a wider view in opening consciousness to the realization that God is as much the life, the Soul, and the Spirit of our neighbor as of ourselves. The moment we begin to see God as the animating principle of *all* men, we are loving our neighbor as ourselves. The moment we can accept the government of God for friend and foe, saint and sinner, we are loving our neighbor as ourselves. But when we make excuses and exceptions we are not fooling the law of God. We are fooling only ourselves, because there is no such thing as release from a violation of the law of God until the violation ceases.

As we study the Master's teaching in the Gospels, we find these laws of love and forgiveness and also the law of service. "For I was an hungered, and ye gave me meat: I was thirsty, and ye gave me drink: I was a stranger, and ye took me in: Naked, and ye clothed me: I was sick, and ye visited me: I was in prison, and ye came unto me. . . . Lord, when saw we thee an hungered, and fed *thee?* or thirsty, and gave *thee* drink? When saw we thee a stranger, and took *thee* in? or naked, and clothed *thee?* Or when saw we thee sick, or in prison, and came unto *thee?* . . . Inasmuch as ye have done it unto one of the least of these my brethren, ye have done it unto me." Service is a law of God.

"Thou shalt love the Lord thy God with all thy heart, and with all thy soul, and with all thy mind." Is there any way to love God except by loving man? If we say that we love God whom we have *not* seen, but do not love man whom we *have* seen, Scripture says that we are a liar. Therefore, the only way we can love God with our whole heart and soul, with our whole mind, body, and being, is by loving man. That love is made manifest not only in the service we give to man, the kindness and forgiveness, but also in our spiritual realization of God as the sum total of individual man's being. The more we can realize God to be the law of our neighbor, God to be the Soul, Substance, and governing Influence, the supporting and supplying Principle of our fellow man, the more we are loving our neighbor as ourselves, and at the same time loving God.

When considering any of the discords and inharmonies in our present experience, let us think now about God as Law, and see if we are violating any law of God. If we discover that we have not sufficiently kept the law of love or the law of forgiveness, we should not be too critical of ourselves, but acknowledge that that is where we have fallen down and, at this moment, recognize that inasmuch as God is the Soul of every individual, we have nothing to forgive; and, moreover, that had not something in our own consciousness attracted this inharmony, it could not have happened. That is the greatest act of forgiveness there is and brings the greatest release. Instead of indulging self-condemnation for the faults we detect in ourselves, instead of judging ourselves for the violation of God's laws, let us, rather, begin at once to realize that God *is* the law unto our being, and that any reliance or faith in any law apart from God—mortal, material, health, or medical law—has just represented our ignorance of the true law.

Now we come to one of the most important laws we shall ever meet: There is no such time as yesterday! There is no such thing as a penalty for yesterday's error. The only penalty is for the error of *this* minute. If at this minute we are placing faith in material law, then we are at this minute paying the penalty for that faith. If at this moment we are not exercising the law of forgiveness, it is at *this* moment that we are under penalty. It is only for the sins of this moment, never the sins of yesterday, since there *is* no yesterday, and therefore nothing that happened yesterday has any place in our experience of today.

Only if our yesterdays were made up of a reliance on spiritual law, do we reap today the benefits of spiritual law. *That* is the only time that *yesterday* becomes a living, vital part of today. The spiritual sowing that we did yesterday is giving us our spiritual, harmonious reaping of today and tomorrow. The material sowing of yesterday has no power except as we carry over that ignorance of

yesterday into today. Two times two is four. There may
have been a thousand yesterdays in which we believed
that two times two is five, but there is no penalty once
we recognize and acknowledge our mistake. Every penalty for our ignorance of yesterday, every penalty for material sowing, is wiped out in the moment of recognition
that the law of God is our governing influence.

At any given moment, we can begin our spiritual sowing, and at the very next moment begin spiritual reaping,
because in Christ there are not "four months" to the
harvest. In Christ, the crop is in the ground before the
seed is planted. "Before they call, I will answer; and
while they are yet speaking, I will hear." The spiritual
reaping begins at the very moment we recognize Spirit
as the governing influence of our lives. No longer will we
be bound by material or mortal law, or even the human
law of doing good for good and evil for evil: Our existence will be one of freedom from bondage and penalty.

The Master gave still another law of God when he
said, "Whatsoever thou shalt bind on earth shall be
bound in heaven: and whatsoever thou shalt loose on
earth shall be loosed in heaven." In holding anyone or
anything in condemnation you are binding yourself in
condemnation. Realize that you are a complete and perfect unit, consciously one with the Father, and all that
the Father has is finding an outlet, through you, to the
world. Be satisfied to see that good flow to the sinner as
well as to the saint. Hold no one in bondage; set everyone free, and you will find your freedom in God, in
Christ. By recognizing God as the source of your life, of
the qualities and activities of your body, the source of

your love and supply, even the source of your powers of forgiveness, you are sowing to the Spirit. But remember that every time you entertain some faith or fear in the creature, you are, in that degree, denying the power of the Creator and, in that degree, sowing to the flesh.

You are called upon to place your hope, your faith, your reliance, your confidence, and your *allness* in the Spirit, in the Infinite Invisible, instead of in the many forms in which the Invisible appears. As you learn to withdraw your faith and your fear from the external world and place your entire confidence in the Infinite Invisible, you are sowing to the Spirit and you truly will reap life everlasting.

As you ponder the idea of God as Law, you will see that there is no way of *appealing* to God or *praying* to God, expecting some benefit *from* God. That would be a violation of spiritual law, and even God cannot violate His own law.

So we must learn not to try to bring God down to *us*, to mold God to our will and whim, but rather must we seek to understand His law and will and bring ourselves into harmony with it. As Abraham Lincoln once stated, "I am not so much concerned as to whether God is on my side as I am in being sure that I am on God's side." So it is with us. Let us not be concerned with bringing the power of God into our experience, but let us be concerned with understanding the law and the will of God, and bringing ourselves into harmony with it.

CHAPTER VI

I AM THE VINE

Somewhere back in the days of our old theological beliefs, we were under the impression that God's goodness to us depended upon our being worthy or deserving, and that if we were bad or had sinned, God withheld our good. If anything should be clear to those on the spiritual Path it is this: God is *love*, God is *law*, God is *principle*, God is *divine intelligence*, and God is *eternal life*.

If life were dependent upon our virtue, and if our badness could interfere with life, or if anything at all could touch the harmonious flow of life, what would become of the spiritual teaching that life is eternal and immortal? Does it say anything about life's being immortal *if, when, and as, we do certain things?* No! That would make immortal life dependent upon you and me, and it is not. Immortal life is dependent upon God, and there is nothing we can do to earn it, and there is nothing we can do to cause God to withhold it. We cannot pray to God to give us life, and there is no sin that can prevent the immortality and eternality of life.

God is love. What, then, could you or I do to change the nature of God? Could our own child do anything that would change *our* love for him? No, of course not, and if, from the human standpoint, we are able to give love to our children often when they do not deserve it, *how much more love* is pouring forth from our heavenly Father!

Can we accept the fact that *God is love*, not God is love if we behave in a certain way, or not just when we are worthy and deserving? Can we accept the fact that *God is love*, and that God's rain falls on the just and the unjust alike? Did the Master, Christ Jesus, withhold good or healing because somebody was a sinner? Did he at any time ask the multitudes if they were good or if they squandered their money or saved it? In raising the dead did he ask if that person had been moral or immoral, honest or dishonest? Or did he, in beholding what the world calls death, destroy all belief in it by raising the individual to life? We all know the answer to that. At no time in his ministry did Jesus withhold healing, supply, forgiveness, restoration, or reformation because of anyone's unworthiness or temporary sense of evil.

The principle is this: Since *God is love*, our good must be infinite without any ifs, ands, or buts, because God's grace is not dependent upon something that you or I do or do not do. The grace of God cannot be withheld. We can turn the electricity on or off and we can turn the water on or off, but we cannot start or stop the flow of

God. *God is, and God is love* in Its completeness and fullness.

Let us now consider the principle: *God is life.* This does not mean that God is life at the age of six years or at sixteen. *God is life.* Then why is this not so at sixty, ninety, or a hundred and twenty? The reason is that the words "I," "me," and "you" enter the picture, and we say *my* life or *your* life, and immediately we think of the date on a birth certificate. If God is life, of what consequence is the date on a birth certificate? God is the *only* life and that life is infinite. Is it God's fault then if we change or get old or become sick and weak and decrepit? The life of God is infinite, eternal, and immortal, and as that is the only life, we can forget your age and my age.

In the same way *God is love,* so let us forget your conduct and my conduct, because some of us may be good or bad today, some better, some worse. Perhaps some of us were better last year than we are this year, but the love of God for His children has not changed, nor has the power of God been stilled. The right arm of God is mighty; the hand of God is not shortened. *God is power,* but God being good—*God is good power.* Can God then withhold help, supply, or peace from anyone? No, but you and I can block it by bringing in the words "I," "me," and "you." "I" may not be deserving, or "I" may not be ready or have enough understanding, but it is not *dependent* upon my understanding.

As we go into the healing work, the first calls will be for what the world calls "lesser claims," and in a short time we may begin to think, "Oh, I have some understanding," or "I am getting results through my understanding." If we do, we shall never become successful practitioners or teachers, because we can never heal through our understanding. God forbid that God's presence and power should be dependent upon our understanding!

Healing is an activity of the Christ; it is an activity of God's understanding. We have been thinking in terms of my life, my health, my supply, my worthiness, my understanding, and these are not involved at all: *It is God's life, God's health, God's supply, God's worthiness, God's understanding.* The Master made that very clear when he said that of his own self he could do nothing; it was the Father within; therefore, it was the *Father's understanding.* The moment we open our consciousness to the flow of God and stop all this nonsense about our understanding and our good or bad behavior, we can be assured of this: The flow of God will erase and purify whatever of error or deed is in our thought today and will wipe out all penalty for past infractions. We must come into the realization that it is not our understanding that does this, but God's, and we must come out from the old Judaic ideas and beliefs of a God of punishment and reward. God is *not* a God of punishment and reward. *God is love. God is life.*

Every one of us still has some idea of God, carried over from his childhood training under orthodox and theological teachings, to the effect that God's favor can be gained by certain acts of omission or commission. Many still believe that God's favor can be gained by certain forms of prayer, worship, or self-discipline. This is not true. Of this we must be sure: *God is not influ-*

enced by man, that is, God is not influenced by individual you and me. *God is the light,* and if we walk out into the light, we will be in it. God's rain falls, and if we want it we must walk out into the rain. *God is, and God is love.* God is pouring forth Its *infinite* grace, but because of the use of such words as "I," "me," and "mine," we are not accepting it.

We must drop this belief that we play a part in obtaining God's love, God's grace, or God's givingness, and remember that the only part we play is to accept it by opening our consciousness to receive it.

The writings of The Infinite Way contain hundreds of truths, but actually there is only one *truth* that we must know. This one truth is *the nature of God.* Take this one thought into meditation: What is God? What is the nature of God? What is the character of God? What are the qualities of God? What is the true God—not the God we were taught to worship as children, or that we ignorantly worship?

Try to empty the already too full vessels, because they cannot be filled with the new wine. Even if you are seventy, empty your old misconceptions and be willing to begin all over with the admission that you do not know God or you would be showing forth more of God's grace. Forget all that you have thought or been taught about God and start afresh with this question, "What is God?" The moment you begin to realize that God is *love* you will know that that love is flowing, unfettered, unlimited, and free, because the nature of God is infinity.

It would be impossible for God to hand us just a thimbleful of love; it would be impossible for God to give us ninety per cent health; and it would be impossible for God to issue us sixty, seventy, or eighty years of life, although it is true that we are only *demonstrating* a thimbleful of love and supply, and just sixty, seventy, or eighty years of life and strength. It may be perfectly true that there is not much love coming in or going out from us, but that has nothing to do with God. It has to do with the false belief that if only we can find the magic formula, in some way we can *start God's good flowing,* or that for some reason we have *stopped* God's good. Is it not rather fantastic to believe that we should live only sixty, seventy, or eighty years in good health and strength when the only life we have is God, and God's life is infinite and is not dependent upon what we do about it? Life is dependent upon God's ability to maintain Its own life immortally, eternally, and infinitely.

Is it not strange that many have so few of the comforts of life when the Master told us that *Truth is the comforter?* He did not say that God would send a *limited amount* of comfort, but he said *the Comforter, the wholeness of the Comforter.* All this time we have been satisfied with a small portion because we have believed that is all we have earned or deserved.

In making a will, we should not ask how much each one of our children deserves and say, "This one has been fairly good so we will leave him a fair amount, and since this one wasn't very good at all, we will cut him off, but because this one has been very good we will leave him a large amount." No, we should say, "We have three children and we will divide equally among them." How much more bountiful is our heavenly Father, and *how* much less does the Father judge than do we. God is not sitting in judgment or condemnation because of our sins, because the only reason behind our sins, faults, and errors is ignorance.

Are we responsible for our ignorance? No, we have listened first to this one and then to that one, and through a feeling of obedience, loyalty, or fear, we have accepted these false beliefs, but the school of life is open to any of us at any time we wish to begin learning, and in our enlightenment we will find freedom. It is only in ignorance that we find discord, limitation, sin, disease, and death. In our enlightenment we find infinite abundance, freedom, immortality, and eternality, so regardless of what our age may be, remember that there is only one subject on which we need to be enlightened and that is: *What is the nature of God?*

"God is light, and in him is no darkness at all." Can you see God as the *great love of the universe* in whom is no hate, envy, jealousy, malice, revenge, or even remembrance of the past? Can you see God as *immortal, eternal, and infinite Life?* If so, you can bring harmony into your bodies and lives overnight. It is only the belief that you are, or are not, doing something that is causing sickness and sin in the flesh. It is only the *belief* that the error lies within you, and *it does not.* So please try to remember this truth: *Man can never influence God.* God is all good, and God's grace endureth forever.

Eliminate the use of "I," "me," "mine," and center your thought wholly on the word *God.* Ask yourself these questions: Is God withholding any good? Can God withhold? Is there any reason for God to withhold? Does

God have the power to shut off Its own benevolence, love, protection, and care? There is no one on this earth great enough to make God do more than God, Itself, is doing, and no sin great enough to stop God from being God.

In the fifteenth chapter of John, we read:

I am the true vine, and my Father is the husbandman.

Every branch in me that beareth not fruit he taketh away: and every branch that beareth fruit, he purgeth it, that it may bring forth more fruit.

Now ye are clean through the word which I have spoken unto you.

Abide in me, and I in you. As the branch cannot bear fruit of itself, except it abide in the vine; no more can ye, except ye abide in me.

I am the vine, ye are the branches: He that abideth in me, and I in him, the same bringeth forth much fruit: for without me ye can do nothing.

If a man abide not in me, he is cast forth as a branch, and is withered; and men gather them, and cast them into the fire, and they are burned.

If ye abide in me, and my words abide in you, ye shall ask what ye will, and it shall be done unto you.

Herein is my Father glorified, that ye bear much fruit; so shall ye be my disciples.

As the Father hath loved me, so have I loved you: continue ye in my love.

If ye keep my commandments, ye shall abide in my love; even as I have kept my Father's commandments, and abide in his love.

These things have I spoken unto you, that my joy might

remain in you, and that your joy might be full.

This is my commandment, That ye love one another, as I have loved you.

JOHN 15:1–12

Now go back to "I am the *true* vine, and my Father is the husbandman. . . . ye are the branches." In your mind's eye, visualize a tree trunk from which grow many branches. Now, remove the trunk. All that is left are loose branches hanging in space, unconnected with each other and unconnected with anything, each under the necessity of supporting itself up there in the air. This is, of course, an impossibility, and in a short time each of these branches will have used up the little life that was in itself and will have fallen away.

Now, let us restore the trunk of the tree and notice what happens to the branches. We find them all connected with the tree, and the tree itself *rooted and grounded* in the earth, from which *it is drawing into itself* all the elements of the earth. From this great earth in which the tree is rooted, the moisture, sunshine, substance, and minerals of the earth are being drawn into the tree, and all that is necessary for the growth and development of the tree is flowing into the branches.

"I [Christ] am the true vine, and my Father is the husbandman." The Christ is the vine, or the trunk, and we are the branches. Each individual seems to be a branch all by himself, unconnected, separate and apart from every other branch, and each is probably wondering how he can get along by himself. Where does he get his life, wisdom, and supply? What supports him? Each one is hustling along, struggling and striving by his individual efforts for happiness and salvation, as if that struggle would maintain and sustain his life. And here Scripture clearly states that *we are branches, but that we are connected with the vine.* The Christ is that vine, so although invisible to human sense, each branch is connected with every other branch. Not one of us is separate and apart from the other, because we are all connected with the vine. We call that the Christ, the invisible Spirit of God, or the invisible Son of God, and each one of us is connected to the other because of this central vine or trunk, and because we are connected with this central vine, we are less dependent upon our *own* power and strength and wisdom.

Because of this vine there is no need for us to live off one another, or to struggle and fight against each other. *We are united in the vine—we are one in the Christ.*

We are one in the Christ, but we go a step further and learn that "*my Father is the husbandman.*" God, the universal Truth, the universal Life, the divine Mind, the infinite Love, is the husbandman, or the equivalent of the earth in which the tree is rooted and grounded. We are branches invisibly connected to the vine, which in its turn is at-one with God. "I and my Father are one. . . . The Father is in me, and I in him," and so this *invisible Christ*, this invisible trunk of the tree or the vine, rooted and grounded in God, *receives all of the good into it and pours it out into us.* Do you not see that our supply is not dependent upon us, any more than the supply of the branch of the tree is dependent upon *itself*? The branch is dependent only upon its *contact* with the vine, and the vine's contact with the ground, the husbandman, or the Father within.

As a student you are a branch, and when you go to a teacher or practitioner, he may temporarily be the vine, the Christ, but only however *if* the teacher knows that of himself he is nothing but that vine. God, the Father within, is the husbandman, and the teacher is one with the husbandman. In his oneness with God, the husbandman, all the truth, the healing, and supplying power flow from the Father, through him to you.

It was through this realization that the Master was able to feed and heal the multitudes, and it is through this same realization that any teacher or practitioner can be the avenue through which good flows to you. Is it dependent upon you? No. Is it dependent upon the practitioner or the teacher? No. It is dependent upon God's grace flowing through the vine into the branches, and as long as the vine remains rooted and grounded in God, just that long is God flowing through the vine into you.

Please remember that you will not always need a teacher or practitioner to be your vine. That is only a temporary relationship. The Master told his disciples, "If I go not away, the Comforter will not come unto you." In other words, *after* this truth has been demonstrated by contact with a teacher or practitioner, and after you have gained wisdom in the realization that the healing did not come *from* him but merely *through* him, from the Father within, you are ready for the next step.

It is then that you will realize, "The invisible Christ, the vine, is not necessarily a person, not even a Jesus, but the Christ is the very invisible part of me. Therefore, I, as the branch, am connected with this invisible part of me, and it in turn is rooted and grounded in God. *It is the Son of God in me. So, the Christ is in the Father, and the Father is in me.*" That realization is the healing truth.

At this point you may be wondering if there is anything you might do, or not do, that would stop this flow of good. Yes, there is one thing. You can *forget* that there is an invisible vine to which you are connected. You can *forget* that the Father is the husbandman and that all of God's good is flowing forth. You can begin to believe that I am separate and apart from you or that you are separate and apart from me, and that if you withhold something from me you will benefit. "I am the vine, ye are the branches: He that abideth in me, and I in him, the same bringeth forth much fruit: for without me ye can do nothing." *Unless you recognize your conscious oneness with the invisible vine, the Son of God of you, you can do nothing.* You will be purged, and you will be a branch using up its little old threescore years and ten of life, and finally you will dry up and fall off. You are purged, *not* by God, but because you did not abide in God and let His word abide in you.

The moment you set yourself apart as a branch and *forget* your union with the invisible Christ, just because you cannot see, hear, taste, touch, or smell it, and so decide you do not have it, "O ye of little faith," you will be purged. Always remember, even in your direst troubles, in your worst diseases, or in your most dreadful sin, *that you are still connected with this invisible vine, and that it in turn is rooted and grounded in the whole of the*

Father, the whole of the husbandman. The very nature of God prevents God from withholding Its flow into the vine and through the vine into you and me. "If ye abide in me, and my words abide in you, ye shall ask what ye will, and it shall be done unto you." But that does not mean that you are to ask in the sense of "Give me a more beautiful home and a better automobile." No, no, no. You merely have to ask what you will, ask for the continuance of infinite Grace, *ask for the continuous realization of Omnipresence.*

"Ye ask, and receive not, because ye ask amiss." God is Spirit, and one does not ask Spirit for material things, which is just what we do when we pray for *things,* and then wonder why they are not received. It is then that someone might say, "Well, you don't go to church very often, and you aren't very kind or forgiving, and you don't have your dishes washed by noon, so you really are not very deserving."

God is the infinite Father. Think to what degree you are a father or mother, and then think of God as *infinite Father.* God is infinite Father, no respecter of persons, and through the invisible vine is continuously filling us with everything necessary for our unfoldment. "Herein is my Father glorified, that ye bear much fruit." Do you understand the meaning of that? Your Father is glorified *only* in proportion as you bear much fruit, rich fruit. Your Father is not glorified by penny-pinching, or by going into a market asking for the less expensive cuts of meat and the cheapest products. Your Father is not glorified when you have to get along with a third-hand automobile. No, no, no, that does not glorify the Father.

The Father does not require that you have anything in the material realm, but *what you do have of good is but the evidence of the Father's glory and not yours.* If you do have a good home or a good income and begin to believe that you are responsible for them because of your understanding or your personal goodness, be not surprised if you are cut off from them. That would be because you were glorifying your own qualities, your own nature and character, and those you do not possess. "Why callest thou me good? there is none good but one, that is, God," and when you realize that the glory of God is showing forth through this good that has come to you, you may expect even greater fruitage because you have acknowledged the Source. "In all thy ways acknowledge *him,*" and He will give you unlimited and abundant good. "If ye keep my commandments, ye shall abide in my love."

The Master gave only two commandments: One was to love God, and the other was to love your neighbor as yourself. How can you love God except in the realization of God as Love? How can you love God if you believe that He is withholding some good or is punishing you, or doing something that you would not do to your own children? You can love and honor God only if you can see Him as *glorious, infinite life—life unfettered, unhindered, and unaffected by man's virtue or transgression.* To love God and your neighbor as yourself is to visualize that tree, and remember that every branch is your neighbor and that your neighbor is deriving his good *through the same invisible Christ, from the Father, the husbandman.*

It may be necessary occasionally, even while you voice this prayer for your neighbor, that you temporarily lend or give him some of the world's goods in order to help him over an acute stage of lack or limitation, but you will never have to undertake continuously to uphold or support the deserving poor, *because there will be no deserving poor if you love your neighbor as yourself.* Every time you see an individual in some form of sin, disease, lack, limitation, deformity, or even death, just catch a glimpse of your tree and silently realize, "Thank God for that trunk." That trunk unites all in oneness, and enables each one to draw from the one infinite Source, and not from one another. It is then that you are loving God supremely and your neighbor as yourself, because you are knowing the same *truth* about your neighbor that you are knowing about yourself.

The Master was careful to describe "neighbor" so that no one would make any mistake. Your enemy is your neighbor, and therefore, when you pray for your neighbor, be sure to include your enemy, for unless you pray for them that persecute you and despitefully use you, and forgive them until seventy times seven, you are loving only *certain* neighbors, and people have found themselves in a great deal of trouble from doing just that.

"Greater love hath no man than this, that a man lay down his life for his friends." You lay down your life every time you declare, "I have no life—God is my life and God is your life." God is the *only* life, the *only* love, the *only* substance, and the *only* supply. Every time you reach out to Truth, someone is laying down his personal sense of life in the realization that his life, being God's life, is your life. Your life, being God's life, is his life, and it is one life. So, when you give up that personal sense of life and say, "This is not my life, this is the life of God, which is mine," you automatically bid good-by to a sixty- or seventy-year span and are resurrected in the realization of good as the infinity of your life.

In these passages from John is found the true vision of God, the Infinite Invisible, as the Source of all good, which can in no wise withhold any good. Good is forever pouring Itself forth individually in what is called the Son of God, the Christ, which is the invisible part of you, and then, through that invisible you, out into the physical body, out into the mind and Soul and Spirit of individual being, to show forth the glory of God. The branch cannot bear fruit of itself, so there can be no personal goodness, health, or wealth. The branch must draw it through the vine, from the Godhead.

The Master's statement, "Every branch in me that beareth not fruit he taketh away," might lead one to believe, after all, that perhaps God punishes in some manner, but that is not true. If you do not abide in this truth, if you do not maintain your conscious oneness with the Christ within you, and through it your oneness with the Father, you will be purged. It will be you separating yourself from God's grace, and thus being purged, destroyed, burned up, or withered away. To abide in this truth is to live and move and have your being in this consciousness of your oneness with the Christ, and the Christ's oneness with the Father.

This, of course, does not mean that you are connected with people, but connected with the Invisible, so that were you set down in mid-ocean or in the desert, you would be able to say, "Ah, but I am *still* a branch of the vine, and the vine is *still* connected with the husbandman, God, and therefore the place whereon I stand is holy ground." Every time you think thoughts of hopelessness and despair, it is as if you were acknowledging that you are a branch cut off from the vine, and the vine from the husbandman, and that you cannot reach either; yet all of the time *it* is right here where you are. *It* is within you, and *it* is Omnipresence.

"I go to prepare a place for you. . . . that where I am, there ye may be also." You may be wondering, "Where is *I am?*" Wherever you are there is the vine, and the Father, the husbandman—the Father, the Son, and the Holy Ghost.

You must always remember that the husbandman, God, does not give and does not withhold—*It just continually is.* The vine of you, the Christ, is not sitting in judgment, but is here to bless and to forgive, to supply and to love. What was the mission of the Master? "Go and shew John again those things which ye do hear and see: The blind receive their sight, and the lame walk, the lepers are cleansed, and the deaf hear, the dead are raised up, and the poor have the gospel preached to them." The Christ is here to support, supply, maintain, sustain, heal, forgive, and regenerate. It is here to resurrect from the grave and to bring about the Ascension.

There is no word in the entire message and mission of the Master that gives any reason for self-condemnation. "Neither do I condemn thee: go, and sin no more." If you return to the old material state of consciousness and do not abide in the Word, you will be purged again and again. Every time you forget that you are a branch connected with the invisible vine, which in its turn is connected with the husbandman, the Father within, you are committing a sin. You can be a prodigal twelve times if you wish, but you will pay the penalty.

If you go back to the belief of a selfhood separate and apart from God—a branch hanging in space—you will bring upon yourself lack and limitation of supply, health, strength, and eternality, but "if ye abide in me, and my words abide in you, ye shall ask what ye will, and it shall be done unto you. Herein is my Father glorified, that ye bear much fruit; so shall ye be my disciples."

CHAPTER VII

GOD IS OMNIPRESENT

Does the fish soar to find the ocean,
the eagle plunge to find the air. . . .
    FRANCIS THOMPSON, "The Kingdom of God"

For in him we live, and move, and have our being. . . .
                                    ACTS 17:28

One of the first things we have learned in The Infinite Way is, in quietness and in meditation, to give up the search for God in the realization that I and the Father are already one, just as we are taught to give up the search for supply in the realization that all that the Father has is mine.

A recent letter from a student stated that a neighbor had asked for help, and that her first thought had been, "Oh, if I could only know the presence of God," and immediately the Voice said, "Stop seeking; God is already here." Always that must be our first realization whenever we meditate or seek communion with God. Whenever we seek access to God, the very first thought we must entertain is that God already *is* where we are. We should not take the attitude that God is something afar off that we must seek.

Any belief that we must *do* something, *think* something, *pray* something, or even be good or worthy in order to attain God, would separate us from our good experience. We all remember Tennyson's lines: "Closer is He than breathing, and nearer than hands and feet," and so any sense of separation from God would intensify one's problems. The poet's words are true—God *is* closer than breathing—and it matters not whether we are praying, treating, communing, or being good or worthy. The omnipresence of God is a divine relationship that has existed from the beginning of time, and so our work is not to seek God or to try to find God. Our work is the quiet contemplation of God's presence within us, and our prayer is the realization that there is no place where we can ever become separate or apart from God!

"Whither shall I go from thy spirit? or whither shall I flee from thy presence? If I ascend up into heaven, thou art there: if I make my bed in hell, behold, thou art there. . . . Yea, though I walk through the valley of the shadow of death, I will fear no evil: for thou art with me."

It is possible to find ourselves in some sort of hell. It may be a hell of sin or disease, of lack or limitation, but we may be assured of this: We are having that experience *only* because we have accepted a sense of separation from God. The remedy does not lie in searching or seeking for God, but in the quiet contemplation of God as omnipresent right where we are. In the midst of this very sin or disease or lack, in the very midst of this seeming danger, God is present.

Many religious teachings, and even some metaphysical teachings, create the idea that because of sin, or some other circumstance, we have become separated from God. These teachings create the belief that if only we can find God, or some way of communicating with God, our problems can be met. None of this is true. There is only one truth, Omnipresence, and that truth has been revealed, not only for thousands of years before the Master, Christ Jesus, but it was so marvelously revealed by him, that we of the Western world have come to accept it as authority. But even while we accept it as authority in Scripture, we deny it in our own experience.

In the New Testament we read of a thief crucified for his offense, who was taken into paradise by the Master "this very day"; and we read of Mary Magdalene, whom the Master forgave and saved from those who would persecute and punish her. Then we have the example to which very few of us have given any serious thought, and that is, the Master's saying that even the publicans and the harlots would enter heaven before the unbelievers. So, you see, there is nothing that can separate you from the love of God.

Paul is very clear about this in the eighth chapter of Romans: "For I am persuaded, that neither death, nor life, nor angels, nor principalities, nor powers, nor things present, nor things to come, nor height nor depth, nor any other creature, shall be able to separate us from the love of God, which is in Christ Jesus our Lord"—neither life, nor death, poverty, sin, nor failure, nothing in this world or the next, *nothing* can separate you from the love of God. There is no power, and there never has been a power that can separate you from the presence of God, the love of God, and the power of God. But just as it is possible to have a friend, a relative, or a parent, and neglect, disown, or walk away from him, thereby depriving ourselves of his companionship, association, and relationship, so we can entertain this thought of separation, thus depriving ourselves of the presence and power of God. Our friend or relative has not deserted us: We have turned our back upon him. God has never forsaken us, but we have turned from this realization of Omnipresence.

You will find this further exemplified as you study the subject of supply according to The Infinite Way teaching. Supply seems to be a very difficult problem for many people, but in the light of the New Testament teaching, it really should not be, because the Master has given numerous positive Christ-rules for the demonstration of supply. In the statement "Unto every one that hath shall be given" is the selfsame principle which has been our relationship with God from the beginning. Instead of seeking and praying to God, instead of fearing that perhaps God may not help, if you acknowledge the presence and the power, the omnipresence of God, even though you may find yourself in hell or in the very valley of the shadow of death, you will find yourself dwelling in the same Spirit as did David when he said, "I will fear no evil: for thou art with me." Remember this—it is the *recognition and acknowledgment* of the presence of God that *brings* God into tangible evidence, manifestation, and expression.

Since God is omnipresent, all good is right where we are. To admit a lack is to deprive ourselves of the abundance that is already ours, and by admitting the lack we deprive ourselves even of the little that we may have at hand. To acknowledge that we already have all that the Father has, whether or not it is visible or immediately available at the moment, is to acknowledge the truth of "Son, thou art ever with me, and all that I have is thine," and that is enough to enable us immediately to start giving, spending, and serving, and in that release the flow of supply would begin.

On every hand we see the demonstration of supply in nature. Take, for example, a coconut tree: One day the tree is without coconuts, but in a short time dozens have unfolded from within, and the tree is ready to push them out into service so that more can be produced. However, if one were to hang a hundred coconuts on a tree, that would not convince the *tree* that this was its supply, because *that* really is not supply. That would have nothing to do with the tree's demonstration—it would be the demonstration of the one who had the coconuts and hung them there.

When we receive a check, we may think that that is a demonstration of supply. The check, however, is not our demonstration at all, but the demonstration of the one who sent it. He is the one who has demonstrated supply or he could not have given it. No matter how much we receive, we never demonstrate supply because our demonstration of supply is determined by how much we give, how much unfolds from within our own consciousness, and how much is released from within our own being. Many who call themselves Christians have accepted the materialistic view that supply is getting, whereas supply is giving. This is a spiritual law, and its violation accounts for the lack and limitation so many people experience.

The same principle will also illustrate the idea of companionship. Many feel that they have no companionship at all, or at least no proper or adequate companionship. That, of course, could not be true. It may be that at the moment they have no companions, but that can easily be righted the moment the nature of companionship is understood. Companionship is not found in a person: companionship is a quality of your own being. It is not something you can get; it is something you must give, and in giving it, there is a reflex action which results in receiving, or tangibly having. Even if one were alone on an uninhabited island, he could begin expressing companionship, perhaps with the birds or the trees, with the sun and the stars, or even with a sea shell. He could begin by feeding the birds and the fish; he could begin the *giving* process, and even from the remoteness of that barren island, safety, security, and rescue would be achieved, and it would be achieved through the correct idea of companionship, because the acknowledgment of companionship would be an acknowledgment of the presence of that which is not seen. Anyone under the belief that he has no companionship need only begin to express it, finding some way to release it from within his own being, and he will soon find himself adequately companioned.

What we entertain in consciousness is what we will find wherever we go. If we entertain lack and limitation, we will find lack and limitation, even in the midst of prosperity. During the years of the depression, many suffered due to the belief that there was lack. Upon analyzing the situation, however, we found that Maine grew as many potatoes, Kansas produced as much wheat, the South as much cotton, and the hills abounded with as many cattle—but still the people were crying about lack. They were accepting in consciousness the belief of lack and then demonstrating it, and yet there was as much abundance all over the land as there had ever been.

Abundance is now, and abundance there will be, even in the days of the next so-called depression, but that next depression will not come nigh your dwelling place if only you can begin now with the realization that you *will demonstrate what you have in consciousness,* nothing more and nothing less. You will not demonstrate something separate and apart from your own being; you will not demonstrate something you are praying to have come to you. You must understand the omnipresence of God and all good *wherever you are,* and then begin to live out from it as if it were tangibly true. Begin to live out as if you *could* spend that nickel, dime, or dollar in the realization that you are making room for the unfoldment of more *from within.*

You begin this with the realization that God is omnipresent. I know that to many there is no feeling, no awareness, or no sense of God's presence. Many, many people in the human world are living as if they were

completely cut off from God, as if they were getting
along wholly by their own efforts. Many are praying for
God's help, God's love, or God's presence, not knowing
how to find it, because they are seeking it where it is not
to be found—whereas it could be so easily realized by
quiet, peaceful contemplation of the Master's great truth,
"The kingdom of God is *within* you."

The kingdom of God is to be found through meditation and prayer. There are two stages of meditation, each
serving a distinct purpose. The normal or natural man
lives entirely in the external—working and playing physically and mentally. His laws are legal, physical, and mental. His instruction and knowledge come mainly from
persons or books. At some period of his life, however,
an interest in God is awakened, and he finds himself
pondering the significance of this statement, "The kingdom of God is within you." This, then, is his first meditation.

Can you not follow him as he first realizes that a kingdom is a realm in which a king lives, rules, governs, directs, and protects? Ah then, if the kingdom of God is
within me—then God's government, God's law, order,
and wisdom must emanate from *within me.* He remembers now the Master's words, "I can of mine own self
do nothing . . . the Father that dwelleth in me, he
doeth the works." This pondering, cogitating, and meditating reveal that God's *power* also comes from within,
and quietly the reminder comes, "My doctrine is not
mine, but his that sent me," and therefore, wisdom,
guidance, and law must always unfold from within.

A whole new world has opened to this student—the realm of God within himself. As this meditation becomes a daily experience—two, three, and four times a day—an expansion of consciousness takes place, and as more and more of this infinite storehouse of wisdom, law, and power is revealed, he learns to depend less and less on outer forms of force, power, law, and knowledge.

Finally there dawns in consciousness the tremendous experience of understanding that since the kingdom of God is within, and the King, God, is ever within His realm, direct impartation of wisdom, direction, law, and power can come from within; and he remembers the words of the boy Samuel, "Speak, Lord; for thy servant heareth." Consciousness then becomes a state of awareness, attuned to the inner kingdom—the deep withinness—and gradually the student becomes consciously aware of inner guidance, direction, and wisdom. This is the culmination of the first stage of meditation wherein the student receives assurance, confidence, healing, and illumination from within his own being whenever he meditates.

The second stage of meditation quickly unfolds of itself. Here the student realizes an almost continuous attunement within, whether working, playing, or sleeping. Always the inner ear is alert. Always a state of receptivity exists, and at any moment, and finally at every moment, he lives under divine government, the reign of Spirit completely touching every facet of his existence. Now there is no more chance or accident, no more doubt or defeat, because the Soul has so enveloped his being that no other force or power can be found. At this point the student realizes, "I live; yet not I, but Christ liveth in me."

Knowing you are Christians, I would not be writing these things if there were not authority for them in the Master's teachings. The Master never told his people anything that could not be verified in Hebrew Scripture, because he knew that it would be unacceptable to them and they would not be able to understand it. All of Jesus' teachings can be found in the Old Testament, repeated in the same, or similar, words in what we call the New Testament. The two great commandments, "Thou shalt love the Lord thy God with all thy heart, and with all thy soul, and with all thy mind," and "Thou shalt love thy neighbor as thyself," which were the most important to the Master, were both taken from Hebrew Scripture. He also told his followers, "Think not that I am come to destroy the law, or the prophets: I am not come to destroy, but to fulfil."

Nothing in the message of The Infinite Way is radical or extreme, since it has its roots in the Bible. There is nothing radical or startling in admitting that you need not seek God or pray for God to come to you or to help you, but that you need only to acknowledge the presence and power of the Father within. The kingdom of God *is* within you—the Father *within me*, He doeth the works —your Father and my Father. So, instead of seeking and searching and praying to God, go to a quiet, peaceful corner, give up searching and make the acknowledgment, "Here and now, the kingdom of God *is* within me. I have all the authority I shall ever need; the kingdom of God is within me, and my heavenly Father knoweth what things I have need of, and it is His good pleasure to give me the kingdom." In this understanding you do not have to demonstrate supply, companionship, home, or health, but go out and begin to spend—money, time, service, love, or forgiveness. Spending has more connotations than just buying a new hat, a bag of groceries, a car, or a house. We spend out of the abundance and infinity of our being when we give love to someone, when we give forgiveness or a bit of joy.

A great Mohammedan poet, Moslih Edden Saadi, wrote:

> If of thy mortal goods thou art bereft
> And from thy slender store two loaves alone
>   are left
> Sell one, and with the dole
> Buy hyacinths to feed thy soul.

Does it seem strange that of two pennies one should be spent for something as seemingly useless as a flower? If we have only one dollar, let us buy our loaf of bread, but let us also spend some for a purpose that will enrich the Soul. Let us spend ourselves, for that is true spending—much more so than when we spend our possessions. Taking this from the standpoint of either God or supply, we find the same principle, and that principle is Omnipresence.

When we consider the subject of health, we find that we cannot pray for God to give us health. It really does not work, except here and there under some great emotional strain, so praying for health is not often a very successful or reliable practice. When we say that we heal by prayer, we mean something far different than praying for health, and what we mean is this: Since God is ever present where we are, health must be ever present, for all that the Father hath is right here where we are, and if God is health we have health. So again, our work is not attaining or praying for health, but the realization of the health that is already in the midst of us. "Son . . . all that I have is thine," and that would include health, strength, and peace.

Where is the Christ? Where is the Master? Here—not on a crucifix! Now—not two thousand years ago, not dead and gone to heaven, not waiting somewhere to return again! No, no, no! *The Christ is within you.* The Christ is the activity of God in you; the Christ is the love of God in you; the Christ is the Spirit of God in you; the Christ is the truth of God in you—within your very own consciousness. It constitutes your divine sonship. So, if you want *My* peace, the *Christ*-peace, turn within and let it be given you *from within.* The Christ gives you *My* peace, surcease from the problems, the discords, and the inharmonies of the world, and it all comes from within your own being.

This brings us to a very, very important part of this entire subject. Since the kingdom, the *allness* of God, is within you, it becomes necessary that you share it, and here you will learn why it is more blessed to give than to receive. Again we turn to the fifteenth chapter of John, where we find those passages to the effect that you are the branch, *I* am the vine, and the *Father* is the husbandman. As you learn to look within yourself for supply, love, companionship, home, and health, you will find that there is an invisible Presence within you called the Son of God, or the Christ. It is your divine sonship, your divine relationship with God; It is your connecting link with God, and *from* God It draws unto you everything necessary for your fulfillment. Therefore, It says, "*I* am come. *I* am the vine—the vine, your divine sonship within, which has come that you might have life, and that you might have it more abundantly."

Think what a muddle we have made of life by looking outside to friends and relatives, husbands and wives, communities, governments and nations, expecting something from them, when all this time the vine, *I* within you, your divine sonship, is there for the specific purpose of giving you life, and life more abundantly.

In every case of seeming need, we learn to turn within to the Christ, the invisible Presence, realizing that Its function is to give us abundant life. It, drawing upon the Father, fulfills us with everything necessary. Just as a law of nature draws into the tree from the surrounding earth all that is necessary for the tree's development, so does the Christ draw unto us, from the godhead, all that is necessary for *our* fulfillment.

That is the first, but the least part of our demonstration. Now comes the really important part when we bring this Christ-truth into vital aliveness, manifestation, and expression. We have been *receiving* this truth of our sonship, of the omnipresence of God and all good, and we are filled with it. Now the time has come when we must begin spending it, using it, and expressing it.

As we go out into the world, we give up our selfhood

as a *branch*, and we accept ourselves as the *vine*. We recognize everyone we meet as a branch, all members of one family, the household of God, all one in Christ Jesus. In that moment, we begin to let this truth which fills us flow out into expression.

When we behold people in any degree of humanhood, good or bad, rich or poor, sick or well, we immediately realize the spiritual truth of their nature, we realize that in them is this same invisible vine, this same Christ, and that Its function in them is that they might have life and that they might have it more abundantly. Should we see them in physical, financial, or moral lack, we silently know this truth: Right in the midst of them is the presence of God; in the midst of them is the kingdom of God; in the midst of them is the Christ, or divine Son, forever drawing unto them everything necessary for their enrichment, happiness, joy, peace, power, and dominion.

As we live in our homes, in our community, and in our nation, it becomes necessary that we *be the vine*—not openly or outwardly, but silently. That which is whispered in silence will be shouted from the housetops, only we will not do the shouting. It should be shouted forth, shown forth as demonstration. We will not be called upon to voice the truth, except when someone specifically asks for it. We will not go out to proselyte or to reform the world. We will not go out to teach the world the Christian truth, but we *will go out as part of a spiritual underground*. In secrecy and in privacy, we will realize that this truth which we have gleaned from Scripture is the truth about our neighbor and our enemy. Love your neighbor as yourself, love your enemy—pray for your enemy, for them that persecute you and hate you and despitefully use you. Silently and secretly within yourself voice this truth about your neighbor, be he friend or foe, far away or near. That voicing is the acknowledgment that you *have* truth, and because you are acknowledging that you have it and are willing to share it, more will be added unto you.

Remember that as an individual you are a branch, and you have within you this divine sonship drawing unto you all that you need. In your relationship to the world, you now become the vine, and you are the one who is drawing truth from God and letting it flow from you to your neighbors, be they men, women, or children, animal, plant, or mineral. Speak this word of truth to your neighbor. Watch the miracle that takes place in your garden as you realize that it, too, is a branch of the same tree, and that this same Christ, this same spiritual sonship, is feeding every plant and every blade of grass.

Our Master tells us, "Man shall not live by bread alone, but by every word that proceedeth out of the mouth of God," and so it is with our crops, our pets, and our cattle. They also live by every word of God, and we can bring forth greater productivity by silently voicing the truth that they are not fed by fertilizers or grass or oats alone, but by every word of Truth.

I have actually seen in demonstration a herd of milk cows increase their milk production twenty-five per cent simply through spiritual realization. It did not deplete the cows either, because it did not come *from* them, it came *through* them. They were not being fed by fodder alone, but by every Word that proceedeth out of the mouth of God.

Everyone who is familiar with horses knows that the Arabian horse is one of the best breeds, but very few know why this is true, and that even to this day, when a mare is in foal, a man reads to her from the Koran, the Mohammedan Bible. That is the reason for the superior quality of the Arabian horse. It is not that their food or climate is more favorable, but that they are being fed, not by bread alone, but by the word of Truth. The love and truth of spiritual wisdom that are conveyed from the Koran, which really means from the spiritual consciousness of the reader, feeds, quiets, and calms the mare, enabling her to be fully productive in health, in strength, and in well-being.

We have seen in our own experiences that a mother who devotes part of each day to reading the Bible and other spiritual wisdom while carrying her child, finds that she has an easier time; the child has an easier time; and there develops a strong and beautiful bond of love and understanding between them.

Watch the miracle when you introduce the word of God into human consciousness, into child-consciousness, and even into animal-, vegetable-, and mineral-consciousness. Notice the marvelous results that follow. It is literally true that it is much better to have one loaf and a hyacinth than to have two loaves. It is much better to have one meal and a book of spiritual truth than to have two meals. Watch this, because it is a revelation that the kingdom of God *is within you*, and you cannot make it so: You can only come into the realization. No spiritual man or woman who has ever voiced or written what he or she has discovered has said other than that the kingdom of God *is within,* and that through meditation it is discovered there and brought into inner realization. No one has yet found God in a mountain or in a temple, or in a far-off country. No, no, no! Many have found or written or spoken *about* God, but God, Itself, has always been found *within one's very own being.*

CHAPTER VIII

MEDITATION

Meditation is the way by which we attain the kingdom of God, and then life is lived by Grace. The ultimate of meditation is a state of complete silence within. The question naturally arises: For one who has not learned the art of inner silence, how is meditation accomplished? Certain it is that it is not a simple thing to achieve, because it is difficult to still the thinking mind. There is a way of meditating, however, which eventually will lead to a cessation of thought, leaving one in a sublime state of inner quiet. In this sacred and secret sanctuary of one's own being, only those thoughts which are of God enter.

There are many ways of meditating, but it is important for the beginner to avoid trying to accomplish something beyond his immediate understanding. In order to meditate successfully and without having disturbing, extraneous thoughts intrude, the mode of contemplative meditation is simple and will lead the student, step by step, into higher forms of meditation.

In contemplative meditation, the student transcends the desire to tell God anything or to ask God for anything. He contemplates the sun, moon, stars, and tides, and all growing and living things, remembering that the heavens and the earth are filled with everything of which man has need. He beholds all things as emanations of God, showing forth God's glory, God's law, and God's love for His children. In this quiet, peaceful state, the reassuring words of Scripture are fulfilled: "Thou wilt keep him in perfect peace, whose mind is stayed on thee. . . . In all thy ways acknowledge him, and he shall direct thy paths."

When we are in a peaceful, quiet, reflective mood in the country, in the mountains, or by the sea, we become aware of the wonder and beauty of the earth. "The heavens declare the glory of God; and the firmament sheweth his handywork." Often in the evening, out on the *lanai*, I contemplate the number and brilliance of the millions of stars overhead, noticing particularly the constellation known as the Southern Cross. The perfect regularity of its appearance is evidence of a law, an order, and an activity governing this event. So it is with the regular and orderly rising of the moon, the ebb and flow of the tide, and the succession of growing things each in its own season.

Contemplating God and the nature of God's work reveals an infinite law governing this universe, filling us with a peace that eliminates anxious concern. How useless it would be to pray for the Southern Cross to rise in the sky, or to pray for the tides to come in or to go out. Would it not be sinful to pray for flowers to bloom, when, before our very eyes, the mystery of life is unfolding, disclosing, and revealing itself effortlessly? The great prophets of old saw that man need do nothing about these great miracles except behold, enjoy them, and be grateful that there is an infinite Wisdom and a divine Love that has created all these things for Its own glory. This really means for your glory and for mine, because God's only existence is as you and as me!

Certainly, if God has created the heavens, the earth, and the oceans, if God has stocked the earth with its good things, can we doubt for a moment that He created all of this for our use, for our pleasure and expression? The futility of praying or meditating for anything should at once be apparent when we perceive this invisible activity of Spirit, appearing outwardly as the harmonies of life.

As we engage in this spiritual activity of beholding God at work, day in and day out, we are brought to a state of consciousness where thought, of its own accord, slows down and finally stops. Then one day, in a second of silence, the activity or presence of God announces Itself to us, and we know that the kingdom of God *is* within us. From that moment, we no longer seek our good in the outer realm; we no longer feel compelled to depend on persons, things, or conditions.

Human experience takes place in a world of time and space, and this in itself precludes its being spiritual in nature. Therefore, let us remember that meditation may be about anything, so long as it is not of this world.

The universe of Spirit is an eternal activity of God. Anything that occurs in time or space, as we humanly understand it, should not be accepted at its appearance-value. Let us remember that every appearance of human-hood, good or bad, is a mental image in thought, actually without reality, law, substance, cause, or effect. In this recognition, the limitations inherent in the five physical senses begin to drop away. We are enabled to "see" deeper into consciousness and behold that which is—eternity in what appears as past, present, and future. We find ourselves unlimited in terms of "here" or "there," "now" or "hereafter." There is a going in and a coming out without sense of time or space, an unfolding without degree, a realization without an object.

In this consciousness finite sense disappears, and the vision is without boundaries. Life is seen and understood as unfettered form and limitless beauty. Even the wisdom of the ages is encompassed in a moment. This is the reality of immortality seen and understood. It is a vision of life without beginning and without end. It is reality brought to light. In this consciousness, there are no barriers of time and space. The vision encompasses the universe: It bridges time and eternity and includes all being.

This meditation on the activity of God in our experience can be carried on while engaged in almost any human endeavor. Whether keeping house or going to business, an area of consciousness can be reserved for the contemplation of God's presence and activity. It is not necessary to leave the world to contemplate God's grace, but only to take a little time during the busy days and nights to be close to God. Let us lift our thought to God, open our inner ear to hear the still, small voice, and with our inner eye behold the universe of Spirit, even while our physical eyes are engaged in human activities. Then we are in the world, but not of it.

The contemplation of God and of the operation of God's law keeps the mind continuously stayed on God. Quietly, gently, and peacefully, the student is observing God in action on earth as in heaven; he is beholding the very glories of God; he is praising God, acknowledging God; and he is bearing witness to the fact that God's grace is his sufficiency.

Once we come to the realization that God's grace is our sufficiency, we are living a life of continuous meditation. We pray without ceasing and yet never do we desire anything, tell God of any need, or try to influence God in any way. There is no strain, because we are not trying to accomplish or to acquire anything. In the realization that the grace of God, which has peopled this earth and has filled it with all good things for man's use, is our sufficiency in all things, we are in a state of continuous prayer. The wisdom which is of God is our sufficiency; the love which is of God and which meets every need of this earth is our sufficiency.

Our only need is the realization of the nature of God and God's government. The contemplation of this leads to other and higher forms of meditation and on to higher levels of consciousness. Eventually, we are led to that place in consciousness where meditation is a total silencing of thought, a complete state of awareness, in which there is an inner alertness, an inner awakening, a state of receptivity and expectancy, into which flows the realization of the presence of God. Beyond that, we need nothing. It is far better to have that realization than to have the entire world of fame and fortune, because that realization is the source and multiplier of loaves and fishes, appearing as health, wealth, companionship, and recognition. Whatever the immediate need may be, the presence of God is the fulfillment of that need.

In our ignorance we, as individuals, have become separated from the actual experience of God, and so we must ask that God reveal Itself. We must ask for wisdom, for light, for grace; but that is all. This form of prayer is wisdom; but the prayer which is a petition beseeching God for supply, security, or peace is foolishness in the sight of God. Supply, security, and peace are free gifts awaiting only the bringing of ourselves into harmony with God's law.

To review the nature of God's work on earth and to realize that there is an infinite Wisdom and a divine Love governing this universe will bring such a great feeling of peace that we may well wonder what could have given us concern. The mere statement that God is infinite wisdom and divine love will not be of any great value. There must be the actual experience of an inner awareness which comes as a result of this contemplation of God.

As we persist in such contemplation, God will become an experience. We shall be living in the realization of God continuously flowing forth as our experience. With an unshakable conviction, we shall know that the kingdom of God is within us. As a result of this higher state of consciousness, greater harmony of mind, body, purse, family, and community relationships appears in our experience. Let us rest in peace and quiet; let the grace of God fill our mind and Soul, being and body, and with a smile, realize: *Thy wisdom is sufficient for me; Thy love satisfies me; I rest in Thee.*

The only legitimate desire is a desire for a greater realization of God—for the things of God and the thoughts of God. God's thoughts are not our thoughts, but God's thoughts can become our thoughts, if we learn to contemplate God rather than to desire or to expect anything. Expectancy, itself, can be meditation, however, if that expectancy takes the form of watching the tiny bud unfold until it becomes the full-blown rose, of beholding the darkness of the night suddenly illumined by the glittering stars and the soft light of the moon, of waiting for the sun to rise and the fullness of its light and warmth to envelop us. But when expectancy implies that God shall move outside Its orbit to obey our directions, supplications, or personal desires and wishes, then such expectancy becomes a sin. Through meditation, the beauty, activity, abundance, joy, and peace of God's grace reach us. In meditation we are enfolded in God.

God must love His children because He created the whole of the heavens and earth for them—for you and for me. It is more comforting to know that God loves us than to know that we love God. God's love is expressed as our love. Without God's love for us, we could not love God, because there is only one love, the love of God, and all love is of God. This realization of God's love for His universe and for His children is a form of meditation in which there is no desire that God should love us more than He does, no feeling that God should be doing more than He already is doing.

If there is any desire at all it should be that we may more greatly appreciate God's love and what it is doing in our life, in our mind, in our Soul, in our body, and in our purse. Let us ponder the bounties that are on every hand and realize that none of these would be possible but for the love of God for His children. God has given us the sun that we may have light by day and the moon that we may have light by night. He has given us the earth and the seas that we may be fed; He has given us soft breezes that we may be refreshed. God has provided for our every need.

Meditation is a contemplation of the infinite ways in which God loves us and the infinite forms of God's love for His creation. We no longer turn to God for anything except for the joy of basking in His presence, in His grace, and in His love.

We need not be too concerned about our love for God; that will follow in a normal and natural way, and we shall find ways of expressing this love. It is not always those who speak most volubly of their love for God whose love is the greatest. The love of God, realized in silence and in secrecy, evidences itself in deeds of loving-kindness. In God's love, there is no criticism, no judgment, and no condemnation.

In God's love, there are no yesterdays. God's love is flowing now. It cannot withhold itself, nor can it give itself. God's love is a state of *is*, a state of being, and through the meditation and contemplation of God, this love of God permeates our consciousness. It is realized and felt to such an extent that prayer becomes the constant and continuing state of our being.

Prayer is a contemplation of God's love for His kingdom. It is a realization of God's presence filling all space, an awareness of peace, joy, and abundance, an inner stillness and silence, a refraining from thought and desire. Prayer is beholding and witnessing God's grace; it is a realization of *is*; it is the holy contemplation:

Where Thou art, I am; where I am, Thou art. "Son, thou art ever with me, and all that I have is thine." God's grace is my sufficiency in all things; God's love is enveloping me and this universe; God's peace is upon this world. "The Lord is my shepherd; I shall not want." Wherever I am, the Lord is.

Prayer is a contemplation of *is*. God *is!* Life *is!* Love *is!* Joy *is!* Prayer is an outflowing of gratitude that God has given us the heavens and the earth for our glory. Prayer is a heart full of gratitude for the still greater blessings in prayer yet to be revealed. "Thou wilt show me the path of life: in thy presence is fullness of joy; at thy right hand there are pleasures for evermore."

Within every individual, far, far within—deeply hidden behind the mask of personal selfhood—is that part of him which is *in* and *of* God. Actually, it is the God-Self unfolding as individual spiritual being.

This Self is never affected by any experience we may undergo—It is untouched by birth, age, or death. Throughout the ages this Self of you and of me is about the "Father's business," unfolding and expressing in accordance with the divine plan. It never fluctuates or deviates from Its eternal state of spiritual being and appointed work. This Self is our spiritual identity, through which the will of God is forever functioning. God's grace is ever feeding and sustaining it. God is the wisdom, the very Life and Soul of individual spiritual being. God is our true identity and individuality.

The stillborn child, the young soldier killed in battle, the multitudes destroyed by plague or epidemic—none of these experiences ever touches you or me or them. Behind these untoward occurrences, the Self, our true being, remains imperishable and imperturbable, unaware of the hypnotism of mortal sense. Under the spell of hypnotism, the life of the subject continues undisturbed, untouched, and with no knowledge of the antics which the hypnotist induces his victim to perform. Awakening from the trance, the subject resumes his normal life with no awareness of what went on under the mesmeric spell. In just this way, awakening from the sense of illness, lack, or sin, the "I" of material sense is dissolved. I live, yet not "I," not the human sense of "I"; now Christ lives my life.

Now our sufficiency is of God. No longer are we dependent upon any person or condition in the outer realm. God is our sufficiency. We look only to Him, to this "he that is in you," for all that is necessary in our experience. Now we understand that I will never leave you, nor forsake you. Now we know that God is our sufficiency in all things.

The ability to commune with God is given us only by

Grace, as the gift of God. Prophecy and divine healing are also gifts of the Spirit and come into expression as Grace quiets the reasoning faculties of the mind.

Under Grace, being is flooded with light, although not necessarily a visible light; the body is weightless and without sensation; there is a oneness with all life. This is not being a part of nature, or even a part of God, but rather being the very fabric of Life, Itself. Being flutters in the leaves of the tree and is the substance and flavor of its fruit. One feels himself to be of the essence of the sea— the actual rise and fall of the waves, the ebb and flow of the tides, the beauty of the rocks, stones, and coral beneath the waters.

All life is one. The one infinite divine Being surges through all being as one Life and one Love. One Soul unites all creation in Its embrace and is the life of all creation. This Soul is not separate or apart from any form of life. Soul is not *in* any being or form of being, nor is Soul separate from being, for Soul *is* Being.

I am not in the earth, or in the tree, or in the bird: I AM these. I AM the gentle movement of the clouds— yet more, the very fleeciness itself; I AM the brightness of the sun and its movement. I AM the breeze in the air, the swaying of palm fronds—yet the palm itself. I look out from the stars—but being also the sky, I hold the stars within me. Beneath is world upon world within my embrace—while I look out from these worlds to the stars above. I AM the life and color of the jade in my ring, and the consciousness of the organs of my body.

There is no place where I leave off as the life of one or begin as the life or mind of another, because all is one. I flow through all, in all, as all. I AM also the flow. I AM in musical sounds, yet I AM the sound itself. Of all creation, I AM the essence, the fiber, the fabric, the form, the action, the very mind and the very life.

The sun shines, and we say, "It is the sun"—it never says so—*it is*. The trees grow; the stream runs on; the rain falls; the child is born. We say so—they never do!

The immortality of being is so evident that we need not say it is so. The harmony of being is by the grace of the Invisible and is not produced or influenced by our saying so.

Not by our power of thought, nor our strength of will, but by the gentle Spirit, do the birds fly, the fish swim, and the dogs play. By It the moon shines, the tides rise, the couples mate, and the joyous being utters song.

Rest. By the still waters, rest. Lie down. In green pastures, lie down, nor say: "I am resting," or "I am lying down."

"My peace give I unto thee," only do not say it—*let* it be. "Underneath are the everlasting arms," only do not voice this thought—recognize it. "I will never leave thee, nor forsake thee," but say it not with thy lips—acknowledge it.

Do not seek harmony or health, or even God. These are not to be found; they already are. "Be still." Only in deep silence, only in refraining from taking thought, only in the giving up of the struggle for God, for peace, for plenty, for companionship, can these be experienced. Do you "see" what I am saying? God, health, abundance, freedom, friendship—these are not entities or identities—but experiences. And this experience of God is what comes to us, and comes to us only through the process known as meditation.